CW01081679

THE CLASSIC OF TEA

Frontispiece: Silently, silently I steal into my chambers
Deserted.
Deserted and barren is the grand hall.
Waiting.
Waiting for a man who will not return.
Resigned, I go to my tea.

THE CLASSIC OF TEA

Origins & Rituals

BY LU YÜ

translated and introduced by
Francis Ross Carpenter
AND ILLUSTRATED BY DEMI HITZ

THE ECCO PRESS

The Ecco Press
100 West Broad Street
Hopewell, New Jersey 08525

Published simultaneously in Canda by
Penguin Books Canada Ltd., Ontario
Printed in the United States of America

This edition published by arrangement with
Little, Brown and Company.

The photograph on page 47 is reprinted through the courtesy of the
Museum of the American China Trade. The other photographs are
reprinted through the courtesy of the Massachusetts Horticultural Society.

Library of Congress Cataloging-in-Publication Data

Lu, Yü, d. 804
The classic of tea : origins & rituals.
p.   cm.
Translation of Ch'a ching.
1. Tea—Early world to 1800. 2. Tea—China—History.
ISBN 0-88001-416-4

9 8 7 6 5 4 3 2 1

FIRST ECCO EDITION

FOR JO

"... in this fragile moment"

CONTENTS

PREFACE

TEA MAY BE THE OLDEST, as it is surely the most constantly congenial, reminder of the West's debt to the East.

Because tea has contributed so much to our common weal, it seems altogether appropriate that there should be a western-language version of the first eastern book ever written about that goddess of herbs, the *Ch'a Ching* or *The Classic of Tea*. Written almost a millennium before tea was even known in the West, *The Classic of Tea* did not appear until well after a millennium of acquaintance with the plant in China. Tea's antiquity, its essential virtues and its acquired meanings all indelibly stamp the plant and the drink as Chinese. Lu Yü has helped to call attention to its antiquity and virtues, and his essay almost certainly first gave to tea the great meanings that it holds for the East today. Because we in the West have shared in the drink for so long, it is good that we begin to share as well in the literature about the drink and its meanings.

This translation has been undertaken in the fond hope

that its shortcomings will not prevent its adding a measure of understanding between the peoples of the East and of the West. The efforts of the West, especially America, in groping toward a new relationship with China will be attended with success only to the extent that we can achieve a friendship between both peoples founded on mutual respect. But mutual respect is an issue of mutual understanding. If *The Classic of Tea* can contribute in any measure to that understanding, the purpose of this translation will have been served.

Francis Ross Carpenter

Braintree, Massachusetts
1974

INTRODUCTION

THE STORY OF TEA EAST AND WEST

Tea: A Mirror of China's Soul

To THOSE OF US used to thinking of today only as the raw material for tomorrow, Lu Yü's eighth-century *Classic of Tea* is a delicately refreshing suggestion of the importance of today itself. In reminding us of that, Lu Yü, his book and its subject reveal themselves as crystalline expressions of a uniquely Chinese attitude. Tea is, in fact, so integral to the Chinese spirit that it matters little how much is produced or drunk in other countries. It will always be China's drink.

In Lu Yü's China of the T'ang dynasty, the spirit of China and its body of belief were multifaceted, to be sure. But basic to that spirit was a conviction that every phenomenon of life, however small, was of compelling concern. Asked about the Tao — the supreme essence of spiritual reality — Chuang Tzu replied that there is no place that it is not. It is, he said, in the ant, the grass, the tiles and shards.

If the Highest Reality was a part of things so low, it followed that every act of living was an act of celebration in the festival of life. And the Chinese did celebrate life, intensely, passionately and continuously. One scholar has made the point that when Buddhism came to China, one reason that it found so receptive an audience was its doctrine of reincarnation. To the Indian Buddhist, reincarnation was an evil to be prevented. To the Chinese, on the other hand, an opportunity for a second engagement with life seemed a most appealing thought. Such an outlook was fundamental to a T'ang ethos in which every moment in time merited celebration as a part of the thread of life.

This is obviously not to say that the Chinese were an especially happy people. We need only refer to their poetry to appreciate their capacity for keen, deep and unremitting sadness. But surely great sorrow is no more than a reflection of one's capacity for great joy. It seems, at least, to be the case with a great body of Chinese poetry that it is either unabashedly sensual rejoicing in the moment or acute suffering over the evanescence of that moment. Consider "A Moonlight Night" by Liu Fang-p'ing, which attempts to freeze for eternity the coming of spring:

> The night has grown old and the moon
>   only half gives us light.
> The Great Bear is at the horizon, the Smaller
>   already set.
> This is the evening when I can believe in Spring
> As insect sounds filter through the warmth
>   of my window silk of green.

But by the same author and with many of the same images:

Silk windows melt into twilight bronzes at sunset.
In golden rooms bitter tears drop unseen
As Spring skulks away from barren courtyards
Where pear petals fall, blocking the doors.

The joyous welcome to spring is balanced by the melancholy awareness of its impermanence. Every moment of life is life itself; every passing moment is the passing of a life. To the Chinese, it is the moment and the act of the moment that constitute life.

It was thus with tea, and so, said Lu Yü, the act of taking tea must be attended by every device with which the Chinese celebrated life in its other forms. Every tea hour must become a masterpiece to serve as a distillation of all tea hours, as if it were the first and with no other to follow.

And so the act of drinking tea must be attended by beauty. Throughout the book, Lu Yü returns to that theme. The environment, the preparation, the ingredients, the tea itself, the tea bowl and the rest of the équipage must have an inner harmony expressed in the outward form. No matter that a certain porcelain be quite rare or quite expensive, if its color is wrong, it must be banished from the équipage. The tea must be chosen for its delicacy and the water for its purity. Even the equipment for manufacturing as well as that for brewing must reflect no lack of attention. Lu Yü is constantly cajoling his reader to "spruce it up" or to add some ornamentation "by way of decoration."

Another typical extension of the Chinese credo expressed by *The Classic of Tea* is the demanding ritual with which Lu Yü would surround the act of taking tea.

To the Chinese, particularly to the Confucianist, ritual was essential to the good life. It was not an end in itself, but it was — again — an outward form or a behavioral expression of an inward ethic. It was to some extent a reflection of the Chinese belief in the natural order of things. The "kowtow," a *cause célèbre* of so many western confrontations with the Chinese, was a ritualistic expression of such a belief. The younger brother kowtowed to the elder; the elder brother, to the father; the father, as subject, to the Emperor; and the Emperor, as Son of Heaven, to Heaven itself. There was nothing degrading in the act. It was simply ritualistic reassurance that the natural order was still intact.

As ritual was the behavioral expression *of* an ethic, so did it help to intensify one's belief *in* the ethic. Ritualistic deference paved the way for genuine respect. Ritualistic acts of graciousness or politeness showed the path to peace and harmony and love. In many ways, ritual served the same ultimate purposes as law in the West.

To the Chinese, especially the Confucianists, ritual was a step toward freedom and not a retreat. Self-discipline, they would have told us, is the first step toward self-realization. And the imposition of outward forms is the first step toward self-discipline. The absence of form and ritual and rules does not assure freedom to the undisciplined mind. Their presence does not deny freedom, but rather abets its attainment, for the disciplined one.

Neither was it intended as a sterile imitation of past

forms but as a means of finding what past sages had found or at least searched for. Ritual provided the order prerequisite to that search.

By the same token, ritual provided a context in which beauty was possible. The order in the équipage, in the preparation when it came time for tea, in the appointments ritualistically achieved, invited harmony of host with guest and guest with guest. And where harmony is, the Chinese believed, beauty will reign. It is, nonetheless, important to emphasize that ritual practice assured none of those ends. It merely created a context in which achievement of the ends (of beauty, or truth, or self-realization) was possible.

Inevitably, then, Lu Yü insists throughout his work on the importance of ritual when one drinks tea. For him the ritual is decisively important. It is another way of celebrating another act of living. The water must be boiled so that it goes through the appropriate stages. The tea must be tested and tasted before it is selected for steeping. There are nine stages through which tea must pass during manufacture and seven during brewing. There are twenty-four implements and each must be used each time (with a set of closely prescribed exceptions). So important is the ritual that it is better, Lu says, to dispense with the tea if even one of the twenty-four implements is missing. When the tea is plucked, where the water is chosen, who is invited to share the tea are of enormous importance. Lu Yü considered it almost unthinkable that a guest should fail to appear. Should a guest be missing, he warns, the quality of the tea must be such as to atone.

One can find yet another of the traditional parts of the credo in the whole question of moderation. It is to be found both in Lu's advocacy of moderation and in his praise of tea for the moderation it induces. Always sip tea, he advises, as if tea were life itself, and do not dissipate the flavor. Never take more than three cups unless you are quite thirsty, for tea, he says, is the very essence of moderation and helps to still the six passions. In a real sense then, moderation is simply another dimension of the love of order in which the passions are restrained, the "middle way" achieved and the beauty of the resultant harmony revealed. That moderation is more easily attained through gentle tea is one of the reasons that it will always be a Chinese drink whatever its origin.

Finally, and perhaps most important, tea epitomizes the Chinese attitude toward time and change. To the Westerner, life has always seemed very linear. Today must somehow improve upon yesterday and tomorrow must extend and build upon today. The Chinese have taken a more cyclic view of their world. The Westerner has danced to an insistent beat called "progress," the Chinese, to a rhythm of natural movement.

Natural movement had several implications for the early Chinese, none of which denied the fact of change. One such implication was that standstill and rest are a part of change. The growth and development of what is unnatural (and therefore wrong) is not change but its very antithesis. Central to the Chinese concept of change is the idea of return. To get back to the starting point and the source of one's strength was of the essence of change. "Fill a bowl to the brim and you will regret it/A sword too sharply ground will dull," says the *Tao Tê Ching* in a warning not to take progress beyond its natural limits. Even death constituted a return and was a part of the natural order. It was neither to be feared nor opposed but rather to be accepted as a fact of life out of which new life would evolve. When Tzu-lai lay dying, his wife and children were admonished to hush their wailing. "Do not disturb him in his change," said his friend Tzu-li.

Implicit in *The Classic of Tea* is the acceptance of this idea of change. That there must be a time to rest is a lesson taught by nature. We disregard it at society's peril, and Lu Yü understood that. Hence, tea was not just a medicine to banish drowsiness (although he frequently praises it for that virtue). It was a means of helping man return to his starting point — that hour in the rhythm of the day when the prince and the peasant shared thoughts and a common cheer as they readied themselves for their separate lives.

Such are the virtues that Lu Yü finds in tea and it is those virtues that dictate the loving attention he would have his reader give to the moment of tea.

Not everyone in China accepted *all* Lu Yü's ideals. The Confucian, for example, with a prescribed ritual for mourning the dead, would have been shocked at Chuang Tzu who refused to mourn his wife's death, saying only that life had evolved death and he would not impose upon her rest. China and the Chinese were compounded of many parts, philosophically, socially, economically. There were the Confucian official, the Taoist adept and the Buddhist priest; the scholar and peasant, the artisan and merchant; the rich landlord and humble farmer.

Lu Yü did not ignore the differences. Rather he accepted and transcended them. In his treatise, the author, the book, and its subject, which is tea, become more than the sum of all those parts. They are, in a word, Chinese.

Tea until Lu Yü's Time:
The Evidence of Language

MYSTERY SURROUNDS THE ORIGIN OF TEA. The legend, to which most early Chinese readily subscribed, is that it was discovered by an emperor of the third millennium B.C., Shen Nung, known also as the Divine Husbandman. Who indeed, other than this Divine, conceived by a princess under the influence of a heavenly dragon, could have given tea to the world? He is supposed to have been burning a camellia bush, to which tea is very closely related botanically, when he began to marvel at the aroma which assailed him. Understanding its source, he then introduced tea and its cultivation to his people.

Buddhists, both Indian and Japanese, understand the origins differently and give the nod to an early patriarch who fell asleep against his intent. When he awoke, he cut off his eyelids to thwart his enemy sleep. However, when the eyelids struck the ground, tea plants sprang up in their place. Thus was born an antidote to sleep with which one could solace the midnight hours without resort to the rigorous measures of Bodhi Dharma. Even in the myth of its origin, note was taken of tea's sleep-dispelling properties.

Beyond its mythical beginnings, there exists considerable doubt — indeed, controversy — as to when tea was known in China as a drink. The controversy centers around a Chinese character called *t'u* which, except for one stroke, is exactly like the character *ch'a* for tea. *T'u* meant many things when it was used in one of China's earliest books. the *Book of Songs*, for example, "sow-thistle," "smartweed" or "rush." And there is some very strong evidence to support a belief that it was also used to signify tea. The word appears throughout the *Book of Songs* and in other classical texts. For instance: "The *t'u* is as sweet as a dumpling." "The girls were like flowering *t'u*." "Fourth month: Collected are the *t'u*." "Seventh month: Luxuriant are the *t'u*." Appearing in the *Chou li* also is the remark that "the overseer is responsible for gathering ripened *t'u* for use in funeral ceremonies."

Most of the uses of the word *t'u* have been commented upon by later scholars. Chu Hsi (born 1130), for example. says that it is a bitter herb, "whose taste is bitter and its juices acrid and injurious to life." Lu Chi, a third-century commentator, also refers to it as a bitter herb and says that after frost, it becomes sweet and pleasant. He cites the *Book of Rites* which speaks of a suckling pig being stewed and then wrapped in the leaves of the bitter herb.

Translations of the word into English have always seemed a bit capricious. Thus, we find it is sow-thistle when collected in the fourth month, a flowering rush when a simile for girls and smart-weed in yet another context.

There is one other early context in which the character appears. In one passage in the *Book of Songs* are the words: "Who says that the *t'u* is bitter; it is as sweet as the shepherd's purse," so it would seem that whatever its other meanings, the *t'u* did serve as some kind of drink. What more likely than the character it resembled, tea? If that is the case, then tea was known as a drink by at least the sixth century B.C., the latest date that the *Book of Songs* could have been written. It or parts of it may even have been written several centuries earlier.

There is further proof that the character *t'u* was used for *ch'a* (tea). A seventh-century commentator on *The History of the Early Han* (206 B.C.–A.D. 24), Yen Shih-ku, notes that it was in this period that the switch occurred from *t'u* to *ch'a* when tea was meant. Even in the place names, the changeover was made. Ch'a Ling, or "Tea Hills," a place in Hunan Province, was until the Early Han known as T'u Ling. That fact is confirmed in the *Li-tai ti-li chi* or *The Historical Geography* of China.

We can add as well that in *The Classic of Tea*, Ch'a Ling is mentioned as an important tea-producing district. It would appear that tea had been produced in those hills for a long time and that the name T'u Ling was applied to them because of the association with tea. When the character *ch'a* was invented for tea, then the name of the place was changed as well.

Why it was changed we can only conjecture. The most reasonable notion would be that tea was assuming such importance that a new word had to be found to replace *t'u*, which was already doing botanical services in too many other directions. It does seem beyond dispute, at any rate, that until *ch'a* was invented during the Early Han, one of the meanings of *t'u* was "tea."

If so, tea was known in China much earlier than has previously been suspected.

Many other names were applied to tea by the Chinese. They include *ch'uan*, *chia*, *ming* and *shê*. They, along with *ch'a*, seem to have been used interchangeably, although many commentators have attempted to attribute to each of them special refinements not always reflected in their usage. But after the eighth century and the publication of Lu Yü's *Classic of Tea* (*Ch'a Ching*), *ch'a* finally came into common use as the word for tea. Certainly by the time of Confucius, about 551–479 B.C., tea was known as a drink. Its merits were mentioned in at least one contemporary text, that of the philosopher Yen Ying who died in 493 B.C.

From the time of Yen Ying on, tea under at least one of its five names made its way into every Chinese dictionary, the first of which was the *Erh Ya*. That ancient dictionary has been attributed to one of China's most famous folk heroes, the Duke of Chou, who lived in the twelfth century B.C. Later additions were made by a disciple of Confucius, Tzu-hsia, at the close of the fifth century B.C. It owes its popularity, however, to a third-century-A.D. commentator named Kuo P'u who completely reshaped the work, dividing it into some nineteen sections, of which seven treat of natural objects. Some of the plant names in the *Erh Ya* are still in use today although most were unknown even to Kuo P'u himself, who relied on earlier commentaries for most of his information. Tea appears there under the name *chia*, and its cryptic definition is "bitter *t'u*." The commentator, however, leaves no doubt that tea was intended when he tells us that "the plant is small like the gardenia, sending forth its leaves even in the winter. It may be boiled into a decoction for drinking." He also adds that the earliest gathering is called *t'u* and the latest, *ming*.

It is under the name of *ming* that the plant appears in the next dictionary, the *Shuo Wên*, presented to the Han Emperor An Ti in 121 A.D. The *Shuo Wên* definition is interesting because it defines *ming* as the buds taken from the plant *t'u* (by that time there could be no doubt that *t'u* was used for tea). But it would also appear that the Chinese had already found that it is the bud which produces the most delicate flavors and that by taking the bud, one can cause the plant to send off many new shoots, known to us as a "flush."

Finally, tea also finds a place in the so-called *Kuang Ya* or *Po Ya* of the third century A.D. The work, compiled by a man named Chang I, was called the *Kuang Ya* until the Sui Dynasty (589–618) when, because the Emperor's name was Kuang, it was changed to accord with the compiler's title *Po Shih*. The dictionary was not much more than an enlarged *Erh Ya* and has one section devoted to plants. It is there that tea is once again mentioned as a drink of the Chinese.

The evidence of language provides ample proof that tea

and tea-drinking practices were by no means new to the Chinese when Lu Yü wrote *The Classic of Tea*. If it was known as a drink by the time of Confucius, it was probably used to some extent even earlier when the plant and drink were known by the character *t'u*. At some point in the Han dynasty, when a new character was needed to designate tea alone, one stroke was dropped from the character *t'u* to form the new one. It was called *ch'a* probably to approach the pronunciation for the other character for tea, *chia*, just as it resembled *t'u* in appearance.

From the Han dynasty tea appears to have grown in popularity, and by the fourth century A.D. it was in somewhat regular use with certain notable exceptions. (In at least one case the guests of an imperial father-in-law quite regularly feigned some indisposition rather than suffer the tea he set out.) It was also in the fourth century that the notion of the medicinal virtue of tea assumed the force of truth in the minds of the Chinese. It is even recorded that a Buddhist priest prescribed boiled tea leaves as a cure for the emperor's headache.

By the time of Lu Yü tea had become far more than a drug and was a common beverage used by all classes of people. The citations of Lu (q.v., Section VII) are adequate and convincing proof. Further proof of its popularity lies in the fact that, as early as the seventh century under the reign of T'ai Tsung, a new custom began of paying a tribute of tea every year to the emperor. The custom persisted into the Ch'ing dynasty.

Tea soon became so popular that Taoists claimed that it was an important ingredient in the elixir of immortality. The waste of fine tea through incompetent manipulation was considered one of the three most deplorable acts in the world (the other two being false education of youth and uninformed admiration of fine paintings).

By the eighth century when Lu Yü sat down to compose his treatise on tea, the drink had already enjoyed a history of at least fifteen hundred years.

Tea from the T'ang to the Ming:
Its Botany, Culture and Manufacture

LU YÜ GIVES US A GOOD PICTURE, and a beautiful one, of the tea plant and its manipulation. It is perhaps fair to say a bit more about the plant that has been learned since.

We now know that botanists have declared tea to be a *Camellia*, and one of the approved names for the plant in the system of international nomenclature is *Camellia sinensis*. That and its other name, *Thea sinensis*, are equally acceptable. It is a beautiful shrub with a leathery, green and shiny leaf tapering to a spearlike point and of serrate edge. Its flowers consist of six to nine petals of pure white surrounding an effusion of yellow stamens. Left alone, it would grow to a stately fifty feet or more and would live a full seventy years. Sedulous pruning, however, prevents its growth and assures an explosion of leaves or "flush" to make it easy to pluck. Yet even the picking is a challenge to this determined shrub, which continues to put forth new leaves as the old ones are put into the service of humankind.

Breaking soil to receive young plants

If not by Lu Yü's time, then certainly shortly afterward, when his treatise had popularized the plant and its leaf, a body of lore, tradition and mystique began to surround the culture of this "jade queen."

To grow a plant, the seed was to be selected in October. It must, said the Chinese, then be dried in the sun and subsequently packed in baskets, mixed in with moistened sand and covered with a mulch of straw.

Once the seed was ready for planting, it was necessary that it be placed in sandy, even somewhat rocky, soil as drainage is most important to the culture of the plant. Tea will not grow well at all if water is allowed to collect around

Planting the seedlings

its roots. It is for reasons of drainage that tea is generally grown on the sides of hills.

In the second month, the seeds were taken out of their baskets and planted near the roots of trees or in a northern shade. Usually six to ten seeds were placed in holes about an inch below the surface of the ground.

As soon as the seeds germinated, the Chinese began very light watering, trying when possible to use the same water in which rice had been washed. Manuring was begun as well. The dung of silkworms or manure in a liquid state was preferred. Oil-cake and dried fish were also acceptable, although there had always been a suspicion that fish would give the tea an unfavorable aroma.

Chinese writers constantly warn against the dangers of overwatering, as they do against close weeding. They tell us that the weeds provide some shade or allow for dappled sunlight for the seedling, and that, in any case, weeding would do much damage to the fragile roots of the new plant.

Good places to transplant the seedlings were near a bamboo or under a mulberry tree on which silkworms fed. This way manuring problems would solve themselves. The transplanting took place some three months after the nursling had appeared. Only after two years could the plants be weeded and "hilled," that is, have mounds of sand, manure and silkworm droppings built up around each plant. The hills had to be kept high and round for drainage, for it is in the nature of the plant to succumb to attacks from water too near the roots.

As it was hilled and weeded, the plant was initiated into its first obedience course by a severe pruning that took it down to about eighteen inches. If the operation was performed in January, the plant would commence throwing new shoots in February. Enough picking then took place to form the bush, and by November, it was a healthy, mature and cooperative plant of about four feet ready for regular picking.

The pickers were always women, usually girls. For three weeks before the pickings, they were required to abstain from eating fish and certain meats so that their breath might not affect the bouquet of the leaves. For the same reason, the picker was to bathe every morning before setting out.

If, however, we can believe the second stanza of a Chinese ballad called "Plucking Tea in My Spring Garden," bathing was not always a rule that was rigidly observed:

Up at dawn, I push at my hair, dab at my face
Seize my basket and out the door while the mist lies
thick.
Young girls and those no longer so go hand in hand.
They ask: Which of Sunglo's peaks do we scale
today?

There would be several pickings, usually four a year. The first picking took place during the period from the fifth to the twentieth of April. That was always the time for the choicest leaves when the plant had its first and most tender flush. Only the bud and first two leaves were chosen and they still so young that they were covered with a white down called *pai hao* ("white hair"). The expanded leaf, to become known in the West as "Young Hyson," was plucked between April 20 and May 1. That picking was called *yü-ch'ien* ("before the rains"). It is a suggestive name, as getting the tea in before the rain fell was a matter of abiding concern with the harvester. In her ballad, the picker sings:

Two by two, one helps the other strip a branch.
Each warns the other to not be slow
Because of the branch whose buds grow old
And the silky rain that will fall tomorrow.

Manuring and watering the young plants

Picking tea from the newly formed shrub

Later, in the twenty-third stanza, is the eternal lament, "The sky is at its troubled worst when firing time is near."

Firing time was indeed a hectic one and not only because of the fear of rain. Once the leaves were harvested (no matter if it was one of the two early spring harvests, the one in early summer or the last one around September), the household became a scene of unremitting bustle.

Before and during Lu Yü's time, the period after harvest was devoted to the manufacture of brick tea. To make tea in brick, one first pounded the leaves to express their operative constituents and then shaped and pressed them into a mold. After that they were strung and hung up to dry in a kind of drying shed. They were first dried by the heat from fuel that could be either hardwood or charcoal over a pit dug into the ground. The bricks were strung and wrapped and carried in baskets suspended from each end of a pole to users over the breadth of the T'ang Empire.

Even after the T'ang dynasty, the use of brick tea continued, though much abated, as one form of the drink in China. As late as the nineteenth century, eleven hundred years after Lu's time, the process had changed but little. Two pounds of tea dust would be weighed into a cloth and laid on a perforated plate over a cauldron of boiling water. It would then be poured into a wooden mold and a half-pound more of fine dust added. Then the mold would be placed under a screw press and clamped shut. It would stay there six hours before it was removed and stacked in readiness for labeling. After the West arrived in China, the brick tea of Lu Yü's era remained as the favorite of the

Russians, who imported millions of pounds of tea in brick from China, especially from the city of Hankow.

Brick tea fell from favor among the Chinese during the Sung dynasty in favor of a powdered tea that was whipped into a froth, starting what really was a new kind of tea drinking. Perhaps it was inevitable that the romantic, lyrical, delicate tastes of the subjects of Sung should require an equally delicate drink to comfort their leisure hours. Even the names they gave it were as new as the tea itself — "sparrow's tongue," "falcon's talon," "gray eyebrows" or "ear of corn."

If Lu Yü had been the ambassador of robust and hearty brick tea in the ebullient days of T'ang, then the Emperor Hui Tsung (1101–1124) of the Sung played the same role for powdered tea. The slender hand of the Hui Tsung Emperor had already reached into many facets of the cultural life of China. And when he addressed himself to tea, it was to write a treatise which would win the ascendancy for powdered tea. Each of the two champions of tea had perhaps only articulated and codified existing practices. But the very forcefulness had also assured that their tea code would be China's.

After the Sung dynasty, the unhappy Mongol period (1260–1368) seemed to herald the demise of tea, if not as a drink, at least as a cultural force. Marco Polo, for example, a careful and enthusiastic, even awestruck, reporter, scarcely mentions tea, and that only in connection with the tea tax. But if tea practices evaporated with a foreign ruler, they returned with all their old vigor, albeit in a new form, with a new and native dynasty, the Ming (1368–1644).

Preparing to wither the new-picked tea

Rolling and grading the tea

It was in the Ming dynasty that tea habits assumed most of their present forms. Tea began to be taken by steeping the cured leaf in a bowl or cup. Since the leaf would sink to the bottom, there was little inconvenience in drinking the liquor. However, many used a cup with a cover which could be raised only as much as necessary for sipping, thereby preventing a mischievous leaf from intruding upon the content of the drinker. Another favorite embellishment among the wealthy was to use a disk of silver filigree which would fit the bottom of the cup and weigh down the leaves.

As tea assumed its present form, methods different from those of Lu Yü's time began to evolve as well. Further, different kinds of teas befitting new tastes began to emerge. Thus when the West arrived in China and discovered the wonders of tea, there would be three basic choices, black, green and oolong.

Black tea was the result of an induced oxidizing fermentation whereas green tea was prepared without fermentation. In the case of oolong (black dragon) tea, fermentation was encouraged and then quickly halted. Within those bald categories there were many, many varieties depending on the tea's origins, the time of its plucking and the size of its leaf.

With black tea, the distinguishing step lay in the withering. When the leaves were gathered they were allowed to dry in the sun upon flat bamboo trays and were gently tossed and rolled to allow the fermentative enzymes to begin their work. After a few hours, the leaves would be handed to a roaster who would "fry" them in a red-hot pan called a *kuo*. The roaster (whose callused hands disdained the heat) stirred and tossed them in the air until an incense stick used for a timer was exhausted.

The roaster passed the leaves to another specialist whose task was to roll and twist them into a tight ball. The process of rolling expressed even more juices, exciting and accelerating even more fermentation. After several such roastings and rollings, the leaves would be dried over bright but flameless charcoal in a *p'ei-lêng,* or drying basket. The *p'ei-lêng* was shaped like an hourglass with a diaphragm in the center to prevent the leaves from falling into the fire. The long succession of roasting, twisting, rolling and drying finally gave the leaves the shape and temper familiar to us all today.

The process for green tea was not so greatly different. The exceptional step with green tea occurred at the beginning, when fermentation was checked by an immediate and intense firing as soon as the leaves were picked.

With its manufacture, the Chinese tea gardener had finished his task. He had saved the seeds from his heartiest plants, nurtured them carefully and tended the nursling plants until they had become vigorously productive shrubs. He had sent his women out to pick at the proper time; and he, his sons and the help, if there was any, had joined with the women in the manufacturing process.

Now the tea was ready to be drunk. But how it was drunk and the implements used depended upon the era. Tea was always a mirror of its cultural milieu even as it helped to shape that culture.

In the lusty and sparkling times of T'ang when men

drove their mounts night and day to supply an emperor's favorite with the sweet and sensuous fruit of the lichee; when poets died reaching for the moon in mocking waters and when the military gave China an empire of vast proportions, nothing but the heartiness of the stalwart tea in bricks would serve. And no cup, says Lu Yü, would do but the sturdy gray-green bowls of Yüeh. Even the individual trees were celebrated for the goodness of their teas. There was one called the eggplant tree, growing in a deep gully and nourished by water trickling from a precipice. The produce of another was appropriated for imperial use with a special officer appointed each year to superintend the gathering and curing. By the time of the Ch'ing dynasty, tea from certain individual trees could cost as much as 120 dollars per catty.

When the lowering cloud of invasion from the North charged the air of the lyric Sung with uneasy omens, men of rank sought pleasure and escape in an art that told them all was well even though they knew that the end was near. As it was with art so with tea. Nothing served during this time but the bland and gentle drink of powdered tea whipped to an airy froth and served in cups from the Eye-of-Heaven (T'ien Mu) Mountains. The simple lines and lustrous texture of those humble wares of Chien made aristocrats of the bowls when filled with tea. It was a time when writing paper and the brush were as much a part of the équipage as the bowl and whisk; when the ability to compose *ex tempore* a poem in praise of a sunset in the pines or of butterflies or tea was as much a part of the etiquette of tea as the ability to handle the implements of the équipage.

And if tea practices were obscured by the shadow of the Mongols when that mighty host spread across China, they reemerged as the Chinese did with the restoration of a native dynasty, the Ming. Again tea reflected the temper of the time. A sober and inward-looking Ming drank tea steeped in cups from the imperial kilns at Ching-tê Chên. So great was the demand for these cups that ministers risked their lives warning against the imperial extravagance of ordering new tea services almost daily. Tea from old areas assumed new importance as the ruling house sought inward strength through outward pomp. The tea of P'u Erh in Yunnan Province, where entrance was forbidden to strangers, who might come only to the bottom of the mountains to purchase tea, enjoyed its brief moment of triumph. But in the demanding times of Ming, tastes could be momentary, and the green teas of Sung Lo in Chiang Nan might well be the next to attract the attentions of an insatiate connoisseur. Some tea so rare that it was only for the emperor was said to be from mountains so remote that it could be harvested only by provoking the monkeys who dwelt among the rocks. When sufficiently angered, the monkeys were said to have torn off branches from the tea trees and showered them down upon their tormentors, who then stripped the leaves.

Another favorite tea in Ming China was the Fukien tea from the hills of Wu I. A sweeter and lighter drink than that of Sung Lo, it became probably the most celebrated tea of China. It had the power, the Chinese thought, to purify the blood of the ill and renew strength in the debilitated. Because so many temples were raised in the Wu I hills, people even began to believe that the tea itself had super-natural powers.

Tea from different places, tea of different kinds, drunk in cups of pure white or of blue and white or with under-glaze decorations in reds; from cups of sturdy porcelain or transparent eggshell bowls — all to satisfy the unfulfilled hunger of an introspective dynasty — such was the state of tea and tea drinking as the Ming dynasty flowered and fell into decline.

Soon (1644), those cups, that tea, would serve a new Manchu conqueror from the North. Meanwhile, far away in the West, came the first tremors of a mighty swell of energy that would turn ocean barriers into highways. Shortly, the caravels of the Portuguese and the East India-men of the English would commence the fateful journeys which linked East and West. Many ships later, centuries after Lu Yü had made it the queen of herbs in China, tea would win its way into the heart of the West, and the tea-kettle would make company with the cat on the cottager's hearth.

The West Comes to Tea

THE RUMBLES OF THE DESTRUCTION of the Han Empire in the third century were echoed by the crumbling of the Roman Empire on the other side of the globe. As "barbarians" poured across the Great Wall of China, so did "barbarians" throng into Europe across the Danube and the Rhine. In China, the new order adopted and popularized a foreign religion, Buddhism, while in the West Christianity provided the dynamism for what would become a new Europe. The magnitude of the transition from Han to Sung civilization was not unlike that of the passage from Roman to Renaissance times in the West.

Still, the similarities were outweighed by the differences. Basic among the differences was the political expansionism of the West as opposed to an early form of cultural isolationism on the part of China. Different also were their new religions. Buddhism in China preached a message of peace, harmony and nonaggression. It was not so with Christianity. Christianity was quickly stamped with the expansive dynamism of the new West. Never totally absent from that religion was the political character that attached to it, and it follows that most of the earliest western visitors to China were missionaries.

In large part the earliest missions to China were part of an attempt to gain allies against the inroads of Islam. But the Marco Polos, the William Rubrucks, the John de Montecorvinos did little to win friends for the West. All of those adventurers or missionaries in the Mongol period shortly heard the judgment of the great Khan. He told them of his lack of interest in their religion and said that while God had given scriptures to the West, to the Mongols he had given shamans. The implication — that he preferred the shamans — was clear.

It was only in a new Chinese dynasty, the Ch'ing (1644–1911), and under a new western religious order, the Society of Jesus, that Christianity began to make headway in China. Great are the names of some of those disciples of Ignatius Loyola, the greatest being that of Matteo Ricci and those of his disciples, especially Verbiest and Schall. It was the Jesuits who proposed a grandiose plan that would have established a Chinese Christian church using traditional Chinese rites. The plan was scotched by the papal bull "*Ex ille die*" of 1742 and Christian missionaries were shortly thereafter denied access to China.

While a good part of the reason for the expulsion of Christians was their own doctrinal disputation, another part was the behavior in the south of China of another set of men calling themselves Christians. They were traders who had come for many reasons — greed, adventure, Christian zealotry or patriotic fervor. Those kinds of motivations were the essential elements of the West's first tentative probes into China.

The Portuguese got there first, followed hard behind by the Dutch and the English, Spanish and French. Each year there were more ships and more men and, worst of all, more Christian guns. For the Chinese, it was a dilemma. They scorned these barbarians (whose behavior frequently made the name most apt) who had left the graves of their ancestors in a single-minded search of nothing more than money. They feared them for their guns and for the challenge that their religion offered to China's own traditions. Nevertheless, they needed the profits that trade could bring, for the costs of empire were great. It was also apparent that the door, unopened voluntarily by the host, would be opened with force by the guest. It was obvious that the Chinese door must be opened to those uninvited guests.

The Chinese were determined, nonetheless, that if the door could not be closed, it would be opened as little as possible. And so was devised a plan unique in commercial history, the so-called Canton system.

The Canton system was compounded of two essential features. The first was that foreigners come to trade (the fact was disguised under the word "tribute") could call only at the port of Canton. The second was that they might deal only through a set of merchants, somewhat like a guild, called the Cohong. There were never more than thirteen merchants in the Cohong and yet they conducted all the business with all the foreigners. In this way the Chinese could maintain the air of having nothing to do with the "foreign devil" even as they profited from his trade.

What did the Westerner bring and what was it he sought? He came with much that the Chinese needed little, but in the end he came with specie and with the plant most baneful to trade for the plant most beneficent — he came to trade illegal opium for innocent tea.

Tea and its companion, porcelain, were to alter the social habits of western man.

The Edinburgh Review once said of tea, "The progress of this famous plant has been something like the progress of truth; suspected at first, though very palatable to those who had the courage to taste it; resisted as it encroached; abused as its popularity spread; and establishing its triumph at last . . . only by slow and resistless efforts of time and its own virtues."

So it was with tea when first noticed by Westerners. Certainly it was more suspected than tasted and certainly only its own virtue won the day. It had been noticed as early as the middle of the ninth century by a Westerner, a Muslim named Suleiman, who said: "The people of China are accustomed to use as a beverage an infusion of a plant, which they call *sakh*. . . . It is considered very wholesome. This plant is sold in all the cities of the Empire."

Tea would not be seen again in western literature, except for a passing reference by Marco Polo, until seven centuries later in 1559. In that year a three-volume work was published in Venice, *Navigatione et Viaggi*. In Volume II one Hajji Mahommed is quoted as saying that the drink of

China was called Chai Catai. He says also, "[T]hose people would gladly give a sack of rhubarb for one ounce of Chai Catai. And those people of Cathay do say if in our parts of the world, in Persia, and the country of the Franks, people only knew of it, there is no doubt that the merchants would cease altogether to buy rhubarb."

The next important notice was in 1567, when two Russians carried marvelous stories of the plant back to their homeland after a sojourn in China.

The most extensive notice of the sixteenth century and the first by a western European appeared in *Historiarum Indicarum, Libri* XVI, 1589. Although the work is intended to be an account of India compiled from the information of Jesuit missionaries, there is on page 103 a short notice of China, *"Sinarum regio,"* which speaks of the vegetable products: "They extract from an herb called *chia* a liquor which they boil to drink, in the manner of the Japanese, and which is extremely wholesome. It protects them from pituitary troubles, heaviness in the head and ailments of the eyes; it conduces to a long life almost free of languor."

Tea appears in English literaure for the first time in the English edition, 1598, of Jan Huighen van Linschooten's *Discours of Voyages into Easte and Weste Indies*. Speaking of the Japanese, he reports: "[W]hen they will entertain any of their friends, they give him some of that warm water to drinke; for the pots wherein they sieth it, and wherein the herbe is kept, with the earthen cups which they drinke it in, they esteeme as much of them as we doe of Diamants, Rubies and other precious stones, and they are not esteemed for their newness, but for their oldness."

Father Ricci alludes to tea in several passages in his journals published by Nicolas Trigault in 1610. He attributes Chinese longevity and freedom from serious illness to their fondness for tea.

The first Englishman to mention tea was probably R. L. Wickham, whose other claims to distinction are few. Writing from Hirado to Macao, he begs an agent of the almost newly formed East India Company, "I pray you buy for me a pot of the best *chaw*." His letter bears the date June 27, 1615.

It was not until 1696, with the publication of Louis le Comte's two-volume work on China, *Nouveaux Mémoires sur l'état de la Chine,* that tea receives its long deserved extended description. In it le Comte attempts a serious botanical description, discusses the horticulture of tea and even discourses a bit on the name, pointing out that the name is *ch'a* everywhere but Fukien Province, where it is termed *tê.* His work excited more interest and both Du-Halde and Grossier relied heavily upon him in their great eighteenth-century descriptions of China.

By the time of le Comte, tea had triumphed at last through the slow and resistless efforts of its own virtues. During the second half of the seventeenth century, the leaf made its way in increasing volume into the West and especially into England. There it was marketed as it had never been in China. After centuries of delicate allusions in the prose and poetry of the East's greatest writers, tea was subjected to the banalities of advertising in jobbers' broadsides. The first such appeared in 1658 and said, "That excellent and by all Physitians approved drinke called by the Chineans tcha, by other nations Tay alias Tea is sold at the Sultaness Head a cophee house in Sweetings Rents by the Royal Exchange London." Two years later, Pepys, perhaps the world's greatest student of contemporary manners and morals, was among the first to try it. "I did send," he wrote in September 1660, "for a cup of tee (a China drinke) of which I never had drank before." It was not he, however, but a foreigner from Portugal, the Infanta Catherine of Braganza, wife of Charles II, who popularized the use of tea. Edmund Waller welcomed her and tea in 1663 when he wrote:

> *The best of Queens, and best of herbs, we owe*
> *To that bold nation, which the way did show*
> *To the fair regions where the sun doth rise,*
> *Whose rich productions we so justly prize.*

Only seven years after that poetasterly effort in praise of Chinese tea, the drink crossed the ocean to the New World, and by 1690 two dealers were licensed to sell their tea in public. At about the same time it appeared in Holyrood Palace in Edinburgh and was sold in an Edinburgh *jewelry* shop, so valuable was it deemed to be.

It was the seventeenth century, then, that saw tea become a common import (more often a smuggled item) into most nations in the West. And as is so often the case with those articles that minister most to the comforts of humankind, it became the most heavily taxed. Scarcely had it begun to be imported than duties as high as five shillings per pound plus five percent *ad valorem* ensured that for many years it would be an item of social prestige, available only to the wealthy. Even so, shortly after the turn of the century over a million pounds a year were being imported into England alone.

Tea's popularity as a drink was reflected in the scientific keenness to name the plant and to get a living shrub to the West where it could be studied as it grew. There was great and proper concern over the name. So different were the green from the black teas that most botanists, not knowing about manufacturing methods, convinced themselves that there were two species, *Thea bohea* (black) and *Thea viridis* (green). It would be many decades before the mistake was corrected.

That they should be so easily beguiled was natural, for botanists had only the most meager of descriptions on which to base their conclusions. Chinese travel restrictions and uninformed observation by travelers worked a double mischief in keeping the laboratory scientist ignorant of its nature. Thus the eagerness of the lawmakers to tax the dead leaf was matched by the passion of scientists to acquire a living plant.

Credit for importing the first live plant into the West has normally been given to the celebrated Linnaeus, who is said to have acquired a living one in 1768. Certainly he had a good opportunity to get one, for he had worked out a shrewd agreement with the Swedish East India Company. By the terms of that agreement, each year one of Linnaeus's students was permitted to join the fleet going to China to bring plants and information back for the master's study. Since the student had to earn his own keep, he usually joined a ship as its chaplain. The most celebrated of his students to go, because he wrote a book about it, was Per Osbek. Osbek brought Linnaeus many plants, even more information. But his attempts to bring back the thing Linnaeus wanted most, a tea plant, ended in a tragicomedy of failure. One he got to the Cape of Good Hope, where it was blown overboard. The other, of which he was signally proud, fell overboard in the harbor when the ship's guns fired a salute on departure.

After Osbek, a certain Lagerstroem got a plant to Uppsala, and it was nourished for two years before it was found to be a *Camellia*. On another occasion a true plant made its way there and because of its value was taken directly to the supervisor's room — where it was eaten by rats. Finally, in 1763, under the command of Captain Ekeberg, a Swedish ship made it back to Sweden with some potted seeds which germinated and grew.

Possibly, however, the real credit for the first live plant to reach Europe should go to James Cunningham, a physician who in 1702 visited the Island of Chusan with the English East India Company. His letters describing tea are published in *The Philosophical Transactions* of 1702, volume XXIII, where he wrote some of the best of the early descriptions. He may actually have succeeded in sending back the live plant, for in an index of flora published from 1692 to 1703, there are two items that refer to *Thea chusan*, suggesting that the author, a London apothecary, had seen more than a description of Cunningham's plants. The same author published, from 1702 to 1709, two volumes of fifty plates each in which are drawn the leaf, flower and fruit. That he was in direct contact with Cunningham we know, for he wrote an article for *The Philosophical Transactions* in 1703 giving an account of Cunningham's work. It is notable that another English botanist, Leonard Plukenet, describes a tea plant as well; it is hard to guess where he might have seen it had he not received one from Cunningham on Chusan.

Dr. Lettsom in 1799 also claimed for an unnamed East India captain the honor of bringing the first plant back, saying he "refused to part with either cuttings or layers." However that may be, we are sure that England had a plant in Kew Gardens by 1768, for the *Hortus Kewensis* lists a *Thea bohea* introduced by John Ellis in that year. Finally, it would appear that the honors for the first shrub to flower in England, if not Europe, should go to the Duke of Northumberland. From his plant, by Act of Parliament in 1771, an elegant drawing of the flower was published. It was reprinted in 1799 by Dr. Lettsom.

The interest in scientific nomenclature was echoed in the attempts to find a *popular* name. Since to the Chinese it was known most popularly as *ch'a*, many of the early references were to some distortion or another of that word. We have already mentioned Mr. Wickham's letter, in which he requested in 1615 that he be sent a "pot of the best *chaw*." In 1625 Samuel Purchas's narrator refers to it as *chia*. However, men from the ships which called at Amoy before European traders were restricted to Canton began to pick up the Amoy word, and it was a corruption of that which finally became the western European and New World name for it. Very roughly and with some exceptions, the Chinese word *ch'a* stuck with tea that went abroad via the land route, and the Fukienese word, with tea that went by water.

In any case, when that much was settled, the pronunciation was still in doubt. In the beginning it was pronounced, and sometimes spelled, "tay." Alexander Pope commenting upon Queen Anne's penchant for holding court across a tea table wrote:

> *Thou great Anna, whom three realms obey*
> *Dost sometimes counsel take and sometimes tay.*

It was not until as late as 1710 that the evidence of poetry allows us to believe that the modern pronunciation was generally accepted.

Certainly by the beginning of the eighteenth century tea had attracted the attention of and, for whatever reason, won the hearts of every stratum of society. The scientific, commercial, governmental and consumer worlds had fallen victim to the gentle blandishments of that blameless drink. The tea trade grew apace. Even Linnaeus, whose first interests in the plant were scholarly ones, confessed that his urge to grow tea plants had also to do with commerce. He said that he "looked upon nothing to be of more importance, than to shut the gate through which all the silver went out of Europe." Into England alone tea came in the following suggestive volumes: In 1669, there were 143 lbs. 8 oz.; in

1769, 4,580,000 lbs.; in 1869, 63,000,000 lbs. Many and varied reasons accounted for the figures which grew in those dramatic increments. Tea duties by the mid-nineteenth century had declined and of course population had increased. Vigorous marketing practices kept tea before the public eye. Prototypical advertising agents glorified its merits "for people of quality" as typical consumers succumbed and bought still more tea. Even morality was on its side as temperance workers praised it out of countenance as a proper surrogate for demon rum. Dickens notes the phenomenon in *The Pickwick Papers* when Mr. Weller at a typical meeting comments to Sammy, "There's a young 'ooman on the next form but two 'as has drunk nine breakfast cups and a half; and she's a-swellin' wisibly before my wery eyes."

Although these observations are only suggestive of the many reasons for the explosive growth of the tea trade, it was tea's own merits as the drink of peace that, in the last instance, brought its quick and lasting triumph. So strongly did it grip the popular imagination that with the advent of the clipper era, there was probably no higher drama, no event more suspenseful, than the annual race of the tea clippers home from China. From rural hamlets and bustling cities across the breadth of England spectators came and slept on the docks just to be there when the ships arrived. Some of the tea would be auctioned off immediately, but great quantities were stored for the quarterly auctions. Such auctions were held by "inch of candle," the high bidder at the candle's last guttering gasp winning the tea. The sales in Leadenhall market were remembered for us by Charles

Preparing to transport the tea
from the Wu I (Bohea) Hills to Canton

Knight, and he says that they were anticipated with dread.
The uproar, filtered through thick walls, was still such, says
Knight, as to make a stranger turn and run fearing a riot.

It is perhaps appropriate than there should be so noisy
a finale to its journey before attending some rustic cottager
or lady of fashion, adding warmth to the fire, light to the
candle and cheer to the conversation. It deserved to celebrate; its journey had been an arduous one. Even before
it began its voyage to the West, it had come as much as
1,190 miles south to Canton from the tea country. The tea
had been placed in chests and wrapped in heavy matting,
then loaded onto boats, care having been taken not to load

the chests too deeply lest they strike the sand and the teas get wet. If it was black tea, it was carried to the mouth of a small river rising in the Wu I (Bohea) Hills and descending into one of the world's most breathtaking lakes, Lake Poyang in Kiangsi Province. It would have traveled very probably from Hsing Ts'un in Fukien to the port of Ho K'ou in Kiangsi at the southeast border of Poyang Lake. From there it moved around the edge of that great lake to Nan Ch'ang, the provincial capital. At each of those three entrepôts, duties were levied. From Nan Ch'ang the tea then traveled south down one of the unsung but extensively used rivers of China, the Kan, as far as Kan Chou. Just below Kan Chou were the Shih-pa tan, or Eighteen Rapids, where the teas always faced grave dangers of wetting or even ruination as they were dashed against the rocks. At any rate, if they survived, they continued south and somewhat westerly to a place called Ta Yü on the border of Kwangtung and Kiangsi. For just that part of its voyage the tea had traveled some 1,845 *li* over a period of many weeks. Along some parts of the route the boats had been dragged over shallows; in others, the tea had been divided into smaller boats carrying perhaps only sixty chests each. At times, the tea men had been obliged to wait until the river rose before they could once again proceed.

But the worst was yet to come, for the tea was unloaded at Ta Yü and carried by porters through the mountain pass that separates the two provinces, Mei Ling Kuan (porters were to be had from post houses on either side of the pass). They were carried by the bitter strength of men who labored under their groaning weight as far as Shih Hsing

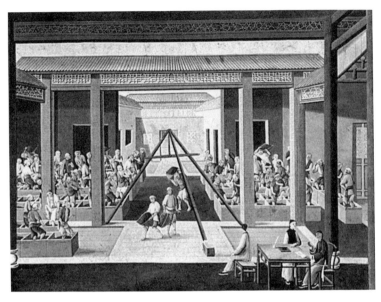

Packing the tea in the establishment of a Cantonese merchant

in Kwangtung Province, where they were reloaded onto small boats for the next to last leg of their toilsome journey. On that leg they went from Shih Hsing to Chiu Chiang, where they were unloaded from the small boats and placed aboard bigger ones capable of carrying from 500 to 800 chests. Those "tea boats" (as they were named by Westerners) then descended the Pei Chiang, or North River, to Canton and the teas were unloaded for the last time before their voyage to the West.

There in Canton samples were taken, and if the teas came up to muster they were loaded onto lighters (called chop boats) and carried to Whampoa where the ships lay strain-

Tea fleet at anchor, Whampoa, about twelve miles from Canton

ing to be off. The typical chop boat was something of a family affair, handled sometimes by three generations in an operation that seems to have been an altogether pleasant way of life. The lading scene is well described by Osmond Tiffany, who tells us that once the boat was ready to depart, the mother would tie a cord around the babies' waists and attach it to an iron ring before settling back to chat, "occasionally enforcing a mild reproof to a vagabond scion, by a tap on the head with a chopstick."

Later on, after the Opium War had opened other ports, the inland voyage was much easier, but there was the same compelling need on the part of the ships' captains to get home where a fortune in prize money awaited; the romance of being the "first tea of the season" commanded exaggerated and outlandish prices.

But neither the rush nor the munificence of the prize justified carelessness in loading. That way lay ruin, for this thoroughbred of herbs was easily hurt. Cavalier treatment at loading assured a ruined cargo at docking. It was a general rule that tea was almost the only cargo, for nearly every other possible cargo was a potential destroyer. No longer allowed were rhubarb, sugar, ammonia, salt, hops, manure, lime or guano. Even silks, a staple in the trade with China, were viewed with hostility by the most fastidious captains. Ballasting became a matter of profound concern. Sandstone, for example, was disallowed. Tea could draw the dampness from anything so porous as that, and most captains preferred to see their ships floored out with boxes of porcelain. They also added to the security of the ship by nailing bamboo over the deck and the side linings while beams were muffled with canvas to prevent leakage into the holds.

Once the tea was carefully loaded (usually by Chinese stevedores, some of the most highly skilled in the world), the race was on. The most intrepid captains would beat straight down the China Sea through the Gaspar and Sunda straits and on past Java Head into the Indian Ocean. Less foolhardy souls stood out farther to the east and dropped down through the Sulu Sea, the Macassar and Lombok straits and thence into the ocean. From that moment until the first chest appeared on the docks, a great part of the western world was alive with the romance of the contest.

The rest of the early story of China's child abroad we

have seen. Its blessings were to be mixed in the future. It may not be altogether uncharacteristic that a simple drink in China whose virtues became the stuff of verse, a subject for painting and an essential feature of the meditative religions should in the West become, in part, an attendant to violence. It was to pay for that innocent plant that the West sought and acquired an empire in the East. It was the proximate cause of the revolt of the colonies in America; and, in a more profound way, the appetite for the profits from tea may well have been one of the prime movers in the colonists' will to revolt.

But if it became a handmaid to violence at the institutional level, the fault was with the institutions rather than the tea. To the drinker it brought the same comforts, the same abatements of the harsher realities of daily living that it traditionally brought to Chinese peasants and philosophers. Perhaps Cowper came the closest in the West to capturing one of the meanings that tea had held for the East:

> *Now stir the fire, and close the shutters fast,*
> *Let fall the curtains, wheel the sofa round;*
> *And while the bubbling and loud-hissing urn*
> *Throws up a steamy column, and the cups*
> *That cheer wait on each,*
> *So let us welcome peaceful evening in.*

The Life and Times of Lu Yü

DESPITE ITS POPULARITY, then, tea never became in the West what it had meant and still means to the East. If it was an extrinsic detail in the culture of the West, it was intrinsic to that of the East. The culture and the drink lived symbiotically, tea acquiring its mystique from the culture as it added new meanings and dimensions to life within the culture.

There can be little doubt that Lu Yü's work was crucial in the development of tea's cultural significance. As the preface to *The Classic of Tea* explains, "Before Lu Yü, tea was rather an ordinary thing; but in a book of only three parts, he has taught us to manufacture tea, to lay out the équipage and to brew it properly." The preface also says that when discussing tea, whether after the fall of the Chou or even in the present dynasty, it is Lu Yü who has every detail. No wonder that sacrifices to him have been made as the god of tea.

So he was a leader in his time who helped create a culture, this man Lu Yü. Lu was born probably in the second quarter of the eighth century and died in 804. His name is an interesting one, for it is closely bound to that most venerated of China's early classics, the *Book of Changes* known also as the *I Ching.*

In addition to the name Lu Yü, his style or fancy name was Hung Chien ("the wild goose advances"). It would seem that he took both names himself after divining one day with the aid of the *I Ching* and drawing hexagram number forty-three, *chien,* or "gradual advance." The hexagram said: "The wild goose [*hung*] gradually advances [*chien*] to the great heights [*lu*]. Its feathers [*yü*] can be used as ornaments."* Thus the surname Lu, or heights, the given name Yü, or feathers, as also his fancy name Hung Chien were derived from his attentions to the *I Ching.* He had many other names as well, having at one time been called Chi with a style name of Li Chi. Coming from Hupei Province in Ching Ling, he was known also as The Scholar of Ching Ling. He liked to call himself The Old Gentleman of Sang Chu (mulberries and hemp).

At some time between 760 and 762, he went to live in seclusion in a place called T'iao Ch'i in Chekiang Province. T'iao Ch'i got its name from the fact that a flower as white as new-fallen snow grows along the bank of the river and

* The hexagram *chien* suggests marriage and the advantages of being firm and correct, among other things. The character for the hexagram itself suggests gradual advancement. It was an auspicious sign, for it also meant — by extension — the advancement of young men to positions of influence and office. The line quoted is the judgment on the sixth line and suggests that he will advance no further, but he may still do good work and justify the ornamental plumes of the wild goose, received presumably from the state. There is more than a suggestion in the passage that Lu Yü had received considerable honor from the T'ang Court (see Müller, Max, ed., *The Sacred Books of the East,* Vol. XVI, p. 180).

in the fall is lifted on the wind until it settles on the surface of the stream and floats away, making the stream look, say the Chinese, as if it were constituted of pure milk. The flower *Lu T'iao* may well have been named for Lu Yü.

Once, it is said, while living there alone, he was walking in the wilderness chanting a poem about a fallen tree. Moved to tears, he came home for tea and wrote *The Classic of Tea*. Although *The Classic of Tea* gives him his present fame, he seems to have produced a wealth of other material now lost. We know, for instance, that Chang Yu-hsin, in a book called *A Record of Waters for Boiling Teas*, cites another work by Lu describing some twenty different sources of superior waters. Some are now so famous that they have been given new names, one in Kiangsu Province having been named Lu Yü Spring.

It is the world's misfortune that they are missing. Even *The Classic of Tea* is available to us now only in editions published as late as the Ming dynasty (1368–1644). At that time, it was included in two different compendia; and its importance was emphasized in 1735 when Lu T'ing-ts'an wrote a ten-volume *Supplement to the Classic of Tea* developing, extending and illustrating the original.

If his writings helped establish Lu Yü as one of the cultural leaders of his time, he was also, of course, a mirror to his own period's exciting history. The fact that he lived in the South where the cultivation of tea was most widespread is important. It may be well to explain some of that background, for it was the South that had reinspired the arts and provided a new context of natural beauty in which sensitive writers immersed themselves with dazzling results.

The last years of the Eastern Han dynasty (25–220) marked a period when artistic endeavor of all sorts was in a considerable decline. It was a time of troubles and internal wars. The petty kings had neither the time nor the inclination to patronize the arts; religious inspiration was almost completely lacking, and the stimulus of Buddhism was yet to come. Confucianism, which had once provided vital and creative answers for past woes, was ineffective in that present crisis.

By 220 the empire had broken down into three separate independent kingdoms, Wei with its capital at Lo Yang, Wu at Nanking and the Shu Han at Ch'eng Tu. For the Chinese this epoch, the Period of the Three Kingdoms, had its own peculiar splendor. It evokes memories of valiant personalities who, like our own medieval knights, have remained popular in the literature which still celebrates their exploits. The names of Ts'ao Ts'ao, Liu Pei and Kuan Yu, for example, are still known by all Chinese, Kuan Yu having been made the god of war.

The Three Kingdoms lasted no more than sixty years, falling after 280 to the Prince of Chin. The Chin period, too, was short lived. By the end of the fourth century nearly all the North had fallen into the hands of a Turko-Mongol people, the Hsiung Nu, or to the Tartars, whose most menacing tribe was the T'o Pa. By 386, the T'o Pa had defeated the Hsiung Nu and established the Northern Wei dynasty. The implication of all this for the art of the period is that it was the T'o Pa Wei, foreigners themselves, who adopted the foreign religion of Buddhism and contributed mightily to its spread both north and south. As we shall see, Buddhism itself would help reshape the South and its art.

As a result of those new incursions, the Chin had moved south by 317. At first, there was much animosity between the upper class of the newly arrived court and the local upper classes. If to that we add the ever-present distrust between the upper class and the peasantry, it is easy to see why controls should have broken down almost completely and why men became relatively free to pursue their individual destinies.

It did not, however, follow that what was bad for China politically was bad for China artistically. To the contrary, the period from 300 on was of immense significance. It was a period when painters as a class began to emerge. Painting drifted away from old styles and the scroll became the new object of appreciation and connoisseurship. Reactions became an artist's own and his statements, personal ones. Belles lettres followed the same paths. Far from being in the service of government or ritual religion, literature began to assume a broader and richer nature, almost any phenomenon becoming fair game for the author.

In another way as well, the forced move south was an auspicious one. The entire area was (and is) one of surpassing natural beauty, with its great lakes, imposing mountains that rise in tapering grace, and, of course, the majestic Yangtze River. No one could have remained indifferent to the delights of such beauty; and Chin artist-poets, Ku

K'ai-chih in particular, caught its spirit in poems of compelling delicacy and in paintings that anticipated the great landscape paintings yet to come.

As the northern kingdoms became more Sinicized and the southern Chinese stronger, the urge toward unification became equally strong. By the late sixth century, China had been militarily reunified and the groundwork laid for the rise of mighty T'ang in 618.

Providing the social cement that had made the issue of reunion easier of solution was the new religion Buddhism. Buddhism in its more contemplative forms and in a close affinity with China's native Taoism afforded a stimulus to philosophical as well as political reunion. For both schools of thought, our "reality," external and superficial, merely served to mask the Tao, the internal and essential reality. One came to profound wisdom, not by rational analysis, but by intuitive absorption into the supreme being, i.e., the Tao. To achieve the state in which such absorption was possible, a state of perfect calm, total equanimity and the absence of effort motivated by personal desire were required.

They taught or relearned the lessons that "there is nowhere that the Tao is not," and that everything we do is an act of living meriting celebration. It was an age of philosophic syncretism, and we were taught by that age that the universal and the particular are one. Thus Lu Yü, born into such an age, found and helped others to find an apprehension of the universal through the particular of tea.

But enough of Lu Yü, the man. It is now time to turn to his book. And as we do, let us approach it as Lu Yü would have wished; and while the teakettle chatters amiably, let us find our own delight in this fragile moment which stands at the crossing of time and space and is a part of eternity.

PART ONE

The Beginnings of Tea

TEA IS FROM A GRAND TREE IN THE SOUTH. The tree may grow from one or two feet to as much as twelve. In the rivers and gorges of the Province of Szechwan are trees whose girth is such that it requires two men to embrace them. Those trees must be felled for plucking.

Its trunk is suggestive of the gourd and its leaves, of the gardenia. The flower is like that of the wild red rose turned white. The seeds are like those of the coir palm. The leaves have the fragrance of cloves while the roots are as those of the walnut.

The character for tea, which we call *ch'a*, is sometimes made with "herb" as the significant element, sometimes "tree" and sometimes both. Its common name is varied with *chia, shê, ming* or *ch'uan*.

Tea grows best in a soil that is slightly stony, while soil that is graveled and rich is next best. Yellow clay is the worst and shrubs that are planted there will not bear fruit.

In planting and transplanting tea, the same techniques apply as for the melon, but the tea may not be picked until the plant's third year. Tea that grows wild is superior; garden tea takes second place. Whether grown on sunny slopes or in shady groves, the best leaves are russet. These are superior to the green leaves. Tea from the young and tender shoots in the plant's first flush is better than that from the buds. The best leaves are those which are tightly curled. Leaves that are open and unrolled are of second quality. Tea picked on the slopes or in the valleys of a sunless mountainside is not worth the effort.

Tea is of a cold nature and may be used in case of blockage or stoppage of the bowels. When its flavor is at its coldest nature, it is most suitable as a drink. If one is generally moderate but is feeling hot or warm, given to melancholia, suffering from aching of the brain, smarting of the eyes, troubled in the four limbs or afflicted in the hundred joints, he may take tea four or five times. Its liquor is like the sweetest dew of Heaven.

One must guard against plucking tea out of season, manufacturing that does not catch its essence or adulterating it with other plants or herbs. Drinking tea under those conditions can only lead to illness.

The injurious properties of tea are not unlike those of ginseng. We know that the best ginseng is produced in Shang T'ang, the medium grades in Po Chi or Hsin Lo while the poorest varieties also come from Korea. Ginseng from Tsê Chou, I Chou, Yu Chou or T'an Chou prefectures is without merit as a medicine. Even worse, if the plants from those regions are not, in fact, ginseng but something like ladybell, they can lead to the six illnesses with no restorative virtue at all.

Our knowledge of the injurious capabilities of ginseng instructs us concerning similar ones in tea.

The Tools of Tea

There are several kinds of baskets, there being one called *ying* and another called *lan*. There are also the *lung* and the *chü*. All of them are made of bamboo. Pickers carry those with a capacity of one to four gallons, or of five, ten, twenty or even thirty pints, on their backs while harvesting the tea.

THE FURNACE AND CAULDRON

Do not use a furnace with a chimney and always select a cauldron with a wide-flaring lip.

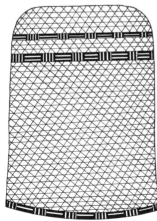

THE BOILER

The boiler, such as one used for steaming rice, and called a *tsêng* is made of wood or earthenware. There is no waist to it but there is also a receptacle made of clay meant to catch droppings from the holes at the bottom of the boiler. The two are joined with bamboo. To begin the steaming, first put the tea in the receptacle. Then pour it into the steamer. Continue stirring it with a three-forked branch in order to spread out the shoots and buds and allow the juices to flow.

THE PESTLE

There is one called *tui*, such as is used in hulling rice, which is perfect, especially if it has known long use.

THE SHAPER

The shaper can be one of two kinds called a *mo* or

mould or a *ch'uan* which is bent in the shape of a basin. They are made of iron and some are round, some, square. Occasionally they are also ornamented.

THE HOLDER

One type is called the *t'ai* or stage. Another is the *chan* or block. They are made of stone but if that is not possible, then from the wood of the pagoda or the mulberry tree. Half of the holder should be buried in the ground so that it will be completely stable during the manufacturing process.

THE COVER

The cover is called *I* and is made of oiled silk or of a single piece of rain gear that has been worn out. To make the tea, place the cover over the holder and then place the shaper over the cover. After the tea has set, it can be moved by lifting up the cloth cover.

THE SCREEN

The screen, called either a *ying-tzu* or a *p'ang-lang* is made from two pieces of young bamboo about three feet long. The body of the implement is two feet, five inches and the handle is five inches. With bamboo strips weave square eyes something like those in a gardener's earth sifter. The screen should be about two feet across. It is used for grading the tea.

THE AWL

Called a *ch'i,* it has a knife and handle made of tough

wood. It is used to bore holes in the tea for stringing.

THE BEATER

It is named *pien* and is made of bamboo. It may also be used to insert into the tea in order to loosen it.

THE DRYING HOLE

To dry the tea, make a hole in the ground about two feet deep, two feet five inches wide and ten feet long. Around the top of it construct a wall two feet high and seal it with wet clay.

STRINGERS

The stringers are named *kuan*. To make them, use strips of bamboo about two and one-half feet long.

Stringers are used to thread through the tea before drying it.

THE DRYING SHED

The *p'êng* or *chan* is a wooden structure built over the drying hole. The wood should be plaited and joined so there will be two stages each a foot high, each in its turn being used in the drying process.

When the tea is half dry, it is raised to the lower stage and as it becomes thoroughly dry, it is raised to the upper one.

TIES

The residents of the land east of the Yangtze and south of the Huai rivers used split bamboo to tie the tea. In the Szechwan mountains, the people make their ties by stringing bark together. In Kiangsu, the largest amount tied together is one catty; a half-catty is the medium size package. A package of four or five ounces is the third size. In the valleys and mountains, the largest load is 120 catties, a medium load is 80 catties and a 50-catty load is the smallest.

In the old days, the character for the tie was the *ch'uan*, meaning bracelet. Sometimes the *ch'uan* of the expression *kuan-ch'uan*, meaning "to string together," was used, but such is no longer the case. The character used now to designate the tie for the tea is *ch'uan*, meaning "to bore through." When it is written, one thinks of the even tone, but it is spoken with a falling tone.

STORAGE CONTAINERS

Storage containers are called *yü*. Their frames are manufactured of roots tied together by bamboo with paper pasted over them. Inside there are horizontal partitions and there is a cover over the top. Below there is a receiving unit at the side of which is a door. Inside one of the door panels is a utensil meant to hold a light fire to keep it warm and dry. In Chiang Nan, in the times of the heavy rains, tea in these containers is specially treated with fire.

The Manufacture of Tea

TEA IS PICKED IN THE SECOND, THIRD AND FOURTH moons. Young and tender shoots, growing on rich, fertile soil, should not be pulled until they look like fern or bracken and are four to five inches long. In any case, the shoots should be picked only while the dew is still cool.

When the tea shoots have flushed out into a thick undergrowth, select the fullest among the shoots of three, four or five branches, pull them off and pluck them.

Do not pick on the day that has seen rain nor when clouds spoil the sky. Pick tea only on a clear day.

All there is to making tea is to pick it, steam it, pound it, shape it, dry it, tie it and seal it.

Tea has a myriad of shapes. If I may speak vul-

garly and rashly, tea may shrink and crinkle like a Mongol's boots. Or it may look like the dewlap of a wild ox, some sharp, some curling as the eaves of a house. It can look like a mushroom in whirling flight just as clouds do when they float out from behind a mountain peak. Its leaves can swell and leap as if they were being lightly tossed on wind-disturbed water. Others will look like clay, soft and malleable, prepared for the hand of the potter and will be as clear and pure as if filtered through wood. Still others will twist and turn like the rivulets carved out by a violent rain in newly tilled fields.

Those are the very finest of teas.

But there are also teas like the husk of bamboo, hard of stem and too firm to steam or beat. They assume the shape of a sieve. Then there are those that are like the lotus after frost. Their stem and leaves become sere and limp, their appearance so altered that they look like piled-up rubble. Such teas are old and barren of worth.

From picking to sealing there are seven steps, and there are eight categories of shapes, from the leaves that look like a Mongol's boots to those that are like a lotus flower killed by frost.

Among would-be connoisseurs there are those who praise the excellence of a tea by noting its smoothness and commenting upon the glossy jet shades of the liquor. They are the least capable of judges. Others will tell you it is good because it is yellow, wrinkled and has depressions and mounds. They are better judges. But the really superior taster will judge tea in all its characteristics and comment upon both the good and the bad.

For every individual criticism there is a reason. If the tea leaf exudes its natural juices, it will be glossy and black. If the oils are contained, then it will appear wrinkled. If it has been manufactured for a long time, it will be black. Tea over which the sun has scarcely set will be yellow. Steamed and tamped, it will be smooth. Allowed to remain loose, it will have hollows and hills. There is nothing unnatural in that, for tea is like other herbs and leaves in that regard.

Its goodness is a decision for the mouth to make.

END OF PART ONE

PART TWO

The Équipage

THE BRAZIER

The brazier should be made of brass or iron and shaped like an old-fashioned tripod. Its walls should be three-tenths of an inch thick at the lip and nine- to six-tenths thick in the body. The brazier should be hollowed out and then plastered over.

On mine there is writing in the ancient script on all three legs, there being twenty-one characters in all. One leg says: "*K'an* above; *sun* below and *li* in the middle." On another leg is the inscription "Cast in the year following the destruction of the Mongols by the Great T'ang." Yet a third inscription says "Harmonize the five elements in the body and you will banish the hundred illnesses."

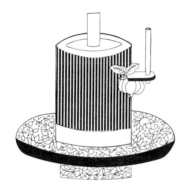

There are windows on my brazier between the legs. The bottom part is the draught hole and the place for taking out the ashes. Above each window are more characters in the ancient script, for a total of six. There are two characters over each window and together they say, "For the Lu family to boil tea."

Set into each window is a grid. One grid has a pheasant on it. Now the pheasant is a *fire* bird. Its trigram is *li*. On another there is a small tiger which is a *wind* beast and has the trigram *sun*. On the third there is a fish, a *water* creature of the trigram *k'an*. *Sun* rules the wind, *li* rules the fire and *k'an* rules the water. Wind can stir up the fire and the fire can boil water. This is why the three trigrams are on it. Other ornamentation includes geometric designs, chained flowerbuds, hanging vines and winding brooks.

The legendary Emperor Fu Hsi inventing the eight trigrams

While most braziers are wrought from iron, they can be made from worked clay.

The receptacle for ashes has three feet with an iron handle for carrying.

THE BASKET

Woven from bamboo, it is one foot, two inches high. It is seven inches in diameter. Some people use rattan and weave it together to make a wooden box in the shape of the bamboo basket. The basket has six openings in it and over the bottom is a cover like that of a satchel added for the sake of beauty.

THE STOKER

It is hexagonal, is made of iron and is one foot long. It comes to a sharp point. On the handle is a small head with a tassel tied to it to set it off. It is not unlike the wooden staffs carried by our soldiers along the dikes.

Following one's own pleasure, the instrument may be represented with the character *ch'ui* or *fu*.

THE FIRE TONGS

Fire tongs were once designated by *chü*, the word for chopsticks. Those in common use are cylindrical and are one foot and three inches long. The head is cut off flush and does not have the onion-shaped head. Tongs with a hook and chain are made of iron or worked copper.

THE CAULDRON

The cauldron is made of pig iron although some of today's craftsmen use the so-called puddled-iron process to make them. They are usually made from old plowshares or scrap chains.

Clay is spread over the inside and gravelly earth over the outside. The cauldron is polished on the inside to make it easy to clean but is allowed to remain rough on the outside to absorb more of the flames.

The ears are squared for stability and the lips flared to facilitate spreading the leaves. The bowl is extended to protect the center. When the bowl is thus extended, the center will be agitated. When the center is agitated, it is easy to toss the leaves. When leaves can be tossed without hindrance, then the taste will be pure and unadulterated.

In Hung Chou the cauldrons are made of tile and in Lan Chou, of stone. Both the tile and stone ones are exquisite utensils, but by their nature they lack stability and are hard to manage. For long usage, cauldrons should be made of silver, as they will yield the purest tea. Silver is somewhat extravagant, but when beauty is the standard, it is silver that is beautiful. When purity is the standard, it is silver that yields the purity. For constancy and long use, one always resorts to silver.

THE STAND

The stand is made in the shape of a cross with the

arms intersecting. It will be scraped down in the center to make a hollow for receiving the cauldron.

THE PINCERS

Pincers are like chopsticks and are made of green bamboo. They are one foot, two inches long. In the first inch, there should be a joint. The pincer should be split just before the joint. Then, when the tea is being heated, sap from the bamboo will drip into the fire. The fire will receive its fragrance and purity and go on to intensify the flavor of the tea. If one is not among the valley forests, then for long-term use, it is perhaps better to use pincers made of purified iron or wrought copper.

THE PAPER SACK

The bag should be made of a paper that is thick and white and made from rattan. One layer should be pressed upon the other and then be stitched to store the heated tea. This will keep the tea from losing its fragrance.

THE ROLLER

The roller is made, by preference, of wood from the orange tree. If that is not available, then either the pear, the *t'ung* or the *chê* should be used. The inner part of the roller is rounded while the outside is square. Thus back-and-forth movement is easily effected without its tipping over. By the same token, the contents on the inside can pile up without spilling over. The shape of the depression carved into the wood is that of the lower part of a carriage wheel without spoke or axle. It is nine inches long and one and seven-tenths inches across. The long diameter of the depression is three inches. The thickness at the center is one inch and that of the sides is one-half inch. The center of the axle is square, and it has a round handle. A brush goes with the roller, the tip of which is made of bird feathers.

GAUZE AND CASKET

The netting or gauze should be measured against the lid of the casket to ensure that it will fit inside. Meant to serve as a strainer, it should be made of fine silk that has been tightly stretched over strong bamboo, split and bent. The casket may be made from a joint of bamboo or from the lacquered wood of the *shan* tree. It should be three inches high, the cover being one inch and the bottom, two inches. The diameter of the opening should be four inches.

THE MEASURE

Sea shells, such as those of the clam or oyster, make proper measures, but it is also acceptable to use ladles made of bamboo, iron or brass. The measure is meant to standardize, to set limits.

To one pint of boiling water add no more than a square inch of tea. If you favor a thin tea, you may lower the amount. Likewise, if your taste runs to a stouter and richer brew, then add still more.

THE WATER DISPENSER

The *chou* tree, the pagoda tree, the catalpa and the *tzu* give up their wood to make the water dispenser.

The wood is joined on the inside and covered over on the outside by sewn cloth or lacquer. The capacity of the dispenser is ten pints.

THE WATER FILTER

Filters in common use are made of frames shaped from raw copper. The use of raw copper will ensure the freshness of the water as well as guard against foul and mossy odors that make the water brackish and harsh. If you use wrought copper, it will smell of moss; and if you use iron, it will create foul odors that make the water offensive to the taste.

People who are tied to the deep forests or who rest in the seclusion of remote valleys frequently make their filters of wood or bamboo. Such equipment does not, however, wear well and for extended use it is best to use raw copper.

There is a bag that fits over the copper frame. To make it, first weave young and tender bamboo together doubled over. Cut a piece of jade-green silk woven with double threads and waterproof and sew it over the copper frame. Ornament it with a decoration of delicate kingfisher feathers or perhaps a silver filigree. When you have completed it, make a green oiled bag to store it. It should have a diameter of five inches with a small handle of only one and one-half inches.

THE WATER LADLE

It is sometimes called a *hsi shao* and is made of a gourd split apart or it may be fashioned from carved wood. A *fu* on tea written by a noble retainer of the Chin dynasty says, "Decant it from the bottle-gourd. Its mouth is broad, its neck thin and the handle short."

During the Yung Chia period, a man from Yü Yao named Yü Hung went into the Pao Pu Mountains to pluck tea and while there met a Taoist adept. He said,

"I am Tan Ch'iu-tzu. May I beg of you the remains of your tea bowl and *hsi*?" The *hsi* was a wooden ladle. Nowadays, ladles are generally made of pear wood.

THE BAMBOO PINCERS

The pincers may be made with wood either from the peach or from willow, grape or palm. It is permissible also to use the heart wood of the persimmon. They should be one foot long with silver set into the ends.

THE SALT DISH

It may be stoneware and if it is round, it should be four inches in diameter. It may, however, be in the shape of a casket, or even a bottle or jar. It is meant to hold the salt. There is a spoon that goes with it, made of bamboo, and is four and one-tenth inches long by nine-tenths of an inch wide. It is like a chopstick.

THE HEATING BASIN

Used to hold the boiling water, it can be made of stoneware or clay. Its capacity is two pints.

THE TEA BOWL

Yüeh Chou ware is best. Ting Chou ware is next best. After that come the bowls of Wu Chou, Yüeh Chou, Shou Chou, and Hung Chou.

There are those who argue that the bowls of Hsing Chou are superior to Yüeh ware. That is not at all the

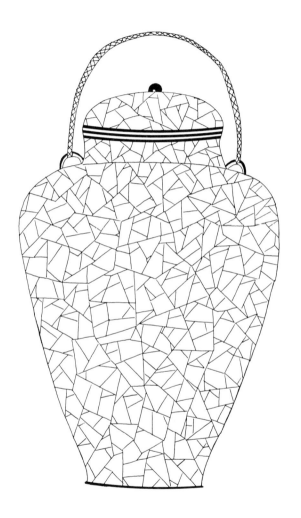

case. It is proper to say that if Hsing ware is silver, then Yüeh ware is jade. Or if the bowls of Hsing Chou are snow, then those of Yüeh are ice. Hsing ware, being white, gives a cinnabar cast to the tea. Yüeh ware, having a greenish hue, enhances the true color of the tea. That is yet a third way to describe Yüeh Chou's superiority to Hsing Chou in the way of tea bowls. In his poem on tea, Tu Yü speaks of the équipage and of a moistly glossy bowl that originated in the East. The bowl was Yüeh ware. Hence for him Yüeh Chou made the best of bowls.

The lip does not curl over, but the base is round and shallow and will hold fewer than eight ounces.

Stoneware from both the Yüeh Chous is of a blue-green shade. Being so it intensifies and emphasizes the color of the tea. If the tea is of a light red color, it will

appear as red in the white bowls of Hsing Chou. If the tea is red, it will look a rusty brown in Shou Chou bowls, they being of a yellow glaze. Because Hung Chou ware is brown, the tea will look black.

All of those are unworthy of tea.

THE BASKET FOR CUPS

The basket is made of white rush rolled and plaited. It is capable of holding up to ten cups. Sometimes a basket like that already described [see page 80] is used. In such cases, paper and cloth are cut, pressed together and sewn into squares for partitions. That type of basket also should accommodate ten cups.

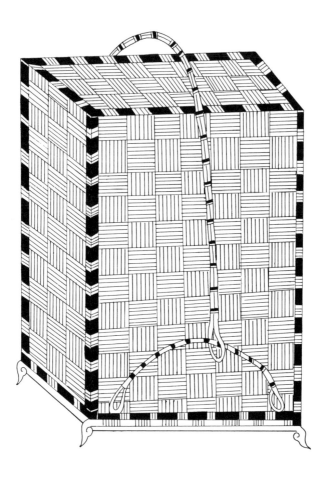

THE BRUSH

The brush should be made by twisting together strips of bark from the coir palm and then binding them together after having inserted them into a block of dogwood. Alternatively, a small bundle of bamboo can be cut and fashioned into a tubular shape like that of an enormous writing brush.

THE SCOURING BOX

The box is meant to hold the dregs after scouring. It is joined together from catalpa wood and then shaped much like the water dispenser. It has an eight-pint capacity.

THE CONTAINER FOR DREGS

All the tea dregs are collected in this container which is manufactured just like the scouring box except that it will hold only four pints.

THE CLOTH

The cloth is made of coarse thread and is two feet long. There should be two and they are to be used in turn for cleansing the rest of the équipage.

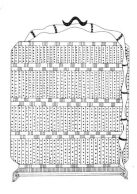

THE UTENSIL RACK

Sometimes it is made like a bed board and sometimes like a rack. It can be built either of the best wood or of unblemished bamboo. Whether wood or bamboo, yellow or black, it can be shaped like the bar to a door and lacquered. It should be three feet long, two feet wide and six inches high. Its role is to hold all the implements so that they can be displayed in their proper order.

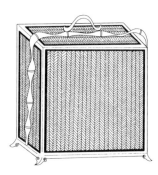

THE CARRYALL

The carryall got its name from the fact that it can properly accommodate the entire tea équipage.

Inside the basket, bamboo slats are worked to fashion triangular or square cubbyholes. Over the outside, double-size laths are used and laid lengthwise across the breadth of the basket. When only single-size laths are used, they should be clamped together into double ones. Into the warp of the weave, cut square holes to achieve an openwork effect. Your carryall should be one and one-half feet high, one foot across at the bottom and two inches thick. Also it ought to be two and four-tenths feet long and open out to two feet wide at the top.

END OF PART TWO

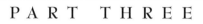

PART THREE

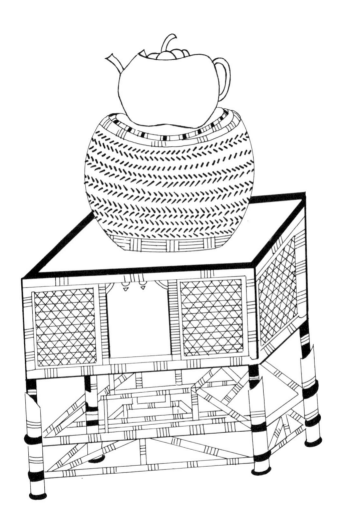

The Brewing of Tea

WHENEVER YOU HEAT TEA, take heed that it not lie between the wind and the embers. The fire can flame out and if it penetrates the brick, the curing operation will be uneven. When that happens, grasp the brick and press it against the fire several times. Then turn it upright until it is roasted. Then pull it out and bank it. When the shape begins to hump like the back of a toad, pull it back five inches from the fire, roll it and let it rest until it assumes its original state. Then heat it again.

When tea is dried by fire, you can tell by the temper of it when it has been cooked enough. When it is sun-dried, its softness will be the test. In cases when the tea is especially young and tender, steam it and then pound it while hot. The buds and shoots will retain

their shape but the leaves should be pulpy. In cases in which the leaves are tough, grasp a heavy pestle and pound the leaves until they are broken like lacquered beads or become like brave soldiers who have received their orders not to halt and go on until there is no strength left in them.

When the tea has been heated until the stems are as tender as a baby's arm, store it in a paper bag while it is still hot. If you do that, then nothing of its original purity or nature will be dissipated. Pulverize it as soon as it is cold. It is best to use charcoal for the fire and failing that, faggots of a very hard wood will do. However, charcoal that has been used before will give off a musty, rank and greasy smell. One must never use an oily wood or worn-out or discarded utensils as fuel.

The ancients placed great store in tea's flavor when it was brewed with firewood that had been cured for a long time.

On the question of what water to use, I would suggest that tea made from mountain streams is best, river water is all right, but well-water tea is quite inferior. (The poem on tea says, When it comes to water, I bow before the pure-flowing channels of the Min.)

Water from the slow-flowing streams, the stone-lined pools or milk-pure springs is the best of mountain water. Never take tea made from water that falls in cascades, gushes from springs, rushes in a torrent or that eddies and surges as if nature were rinsing its mouth. Over usage of all such water to make tea will lead to illnesses of the throat.

Of the many other streams that flow through mountain and valley, there are those that are clear and pure

but which sink into the ground and are absorbed before finding an outlet. From the hot season to the time of frost, the dragon may be sequestered and noxious poisons will accumulate within them. One taste of the water will tell you if it is all right. If the evil genius of a stream makes the water bubble like a fresh spring, pour it out.

If you must use river water, take only that which man has not been near; and if it is well water, then draw a great deal before using it.

When the water is boiling, it must look like fishes' eyes and give off but the hint of a sound. When at the edges it chatters like a bubbling spring and looks like pearls innumerable strung together, it has reached the second stage. When it leaps like breakers majestic and resounds like a swelling wave, it is at its peak. Any more and the water will be boiled out and should not be used.

When the boiling water is in its first stage, you may add a measure of salt in accordance with the amount of water. You can tell when to stop by sampling it.

During the second stage of the boiling, draw off a ladle full of water and stir around the center of the boil with your bamboo pincers. If you judge that it is not yet right, lower the pincers into the center of the

boil and do it with force. If it still leaps up making waves and splashing into a froth, pour back some of the water you have drawn off. That will stop it from overboiling while encouraging its essential virtue.

Pour it into cups so that it will come out frothy. The frothy patches are the ornamentation to the decoction and are called *mo* if thin, *po* if thick. When they are fine and light, they are called flowers, for they resemble the flowers of the jujube tree tossing lightly on the surface of a circular pool.

They should suggest eddying pools, twisting islets or floating duckweed at the time of the world's creation. They should be like scudding clouds in a clear blue sky and should occasionally overlap like scales on fish. They should be like copper *cash*, green with age, churned by the rapids of a river, or dispose themselves as chrysanthemum petals would, promiscuously cast on a goblet's stand.

To achieve the froth called *po*, heat the remaining water until it boils. Then the fine, light flowery froth will gather and become as silvery and white as drifted snow.

The poem on tea speaks of froth as flaming brilliance, and says that it must be as lustrous as the snowdrift and as sumptuous as the spring lotus.

When you draw off the water during the first boil, allow it to stand. If on the surface of the froth there is a lining like a black cloud, do not drink it, for the flavor will be untrue.

The first cup should have a haunting flavor, strange and lasting. There are those who allow it to continue simmering to nourish the elegance and retain the froth even through a first, second and third cup. After the third cup, one should not drink more than a fourth or fifth cup unless he is very thirsty.

At every brewing, one pint of water should be used for five cups of tea. Take the tea cups one after the other so that the heavy impurities will remain at the bottom and the choicest froths float across the top like patches of thin ice. Then the delicate virtues of the tea will be retained throughout. But when you drink it, sip only. Otherwise, you will dissipate the flavor.

Moderation is the very essence of tea. Tea does not lend itself to extravagance. If a tea is insipid and bland, it will lose its flavor before even half a cup has disappeared. How much more so in the case of extravagance in its use. The vibrance will fade from the

color and the perfection of its fragrance will melt away.

When tea has a sweet flavor, it may be called *chia*. If it is less than sweet and of a bitter or strong taste, it is called *ch'uan*. If it is bitter or strong when sipped but sweet when swallowed, it is called *ch'a*.

Drinking the Tea

BORN TO THIS EARTH are three kinds of creatures. Some are winged and fly. Some are furred and run. Still others stretch their mouths and talk. All of them must eat and drink to survive.

There are times, nonetheless, when the meaning of "drink" becomes obscure. If one would merely slake his thirst, then he can drink rice and water. Should melancholy, sadness or anger strike, he can turn to wine to drink. But if one would dispel an evening's unproductive lassitude, the meaning of "drink" is tea.

Now tea, used as a drink, was first discovered by the Emperor Shen Nung. Among other great tea drinkers, we have heard that in the State of Lu there was the Duke of Chou while the State of Ch'i had Yen Ying. During the Han Dynasty there were Yang

Hsiung and Ssu-Ma Hsiang-ju. During the Wu, there was Wei Yao. During the Chin there were Liu Kun, as well as Chang Ts'ai, my distant ancestor Lu Na and Hsieh An among others pulled out of memory at random. All of them drank tea.

Tea has been traditionally taken so extensively that it is immersed in our customs and flourishes in the present Dynasty both North and South. From Ching to Yü, it is the common drink of every household.

The beverage that the people take may be from coarse, loose, powdered or cake tea. It can be chopped, boiled, roasted and then tamped down into a bottle or pottery vessel where it awaits only hot water.

Sometimes such items as onion, ginger, jujube fruit, orange peel, dogwood berries or peppermint are boiled along with the tea. Such ingredients may be merely scattered across the top for a glossy effect, or they can be boiled together and the froth drawn off. Drinks like that are no more than the swill of gutters and ditches; still, alas, it is a common practice to make tea that way.

In the ten thousand objects which Heaven nour-

ishes, there is supreme perfection. It is only for ease and comfort that man works at things. He sequesters himself in a house. So the house he refines to the perfection of his own taste. He covers himself with clothing. The clothing he refines to perfection. He consumes to satiety both food and drink. These also he cultivates and refines to the utmost.

Thus with tea. There are nine ways by which man must tax himself when he has to do with tea.

He must manufacture it.

He must develop a sense of selectivity and discrimination about it.

He must provide the proper implements.

He must prepare the right kind of fire.

He must select a suitable water.

He must roast the tea to a turn.

He must grind it well.

He must brew it to its ultimate perfection.

He must, finally, drink it.

There are no short cuts. Merely to pick tea in the shade and dry it in the cool of the evening is not to manufacture it. To nibble it for flavor and sniff at it for fragrance is not to be discriminating. To bring along a musty tripod or a bowl charged with nose-insulting odors is not to provide the proper implements. Resinous firewood and old kitchen charcoal are not the stuff for a seemly fire. Water from turbulent rapids or dammed-up flood water is not a suitable water. Tea cannot be said to be roasted when it is heated on the outside and left raw underneath. Reducing it to jade powder and green dust is not grinding tea. Manipulating the instruments awkwardly and transitions from instrument to instrument that attract attention are not brewing tea. Finally, taking prodigious amounts of tea in summer and none at all in winter are not drinking tea.

For exquisite freshness and vibrant fragrance, limit the number of cups to three. If one can be satisfied with less than perfection, five are permissible. If one's guests number up to five rows, it will be necessary to use three bowls. If seven, then five bowls will be required. If there are six guests or fewer, do not economize on the number of bowls.

But if even one guest is missing from the assemblage, then the haunting and lasting flavor of the tea must take his place.

Notations on Tea

THE FOLLOWING HAVE HAD TO DO WITH TEA IN some important way.

1. In the Period of the Three Emperors, Shên Nung also known as the Emperor Yen.
2. In the Chou Dynasty, Tan, the Duke of Chou from the State of Lu.
3. From the State of Ch'i, Yen Ying.
4. From the Han Dynasty
   a. The Taoist Immortal, Tan Ch'iu-tzu.
   b. Ssu-Ma Hsiang-ju.
   c. The Minister Yang Hsiung.
5. In the Wu Dynasty, the Kuei Ming Hou Period, Wei Hung-szu.

The Duke of Chou

6. During the Chin Dynasty there were
   a. During the Hui Ti Period, Liu Kun.
   b. His nephew and Governor of Yen Chou, Liu Yen.
   c. The Eunuch Chang Mêng.
   d. Lu Na of Wu Hsing.
   e. His nephew of Hui Chi, Lu Shu.
   f. The General Hsieh An-shih.
   g. Kuo P'u of Hung Nung.
   h. Huan Wên of Yang Chou.
   i. The Nobleman, Tu Yü.
   j. The Buddhist Yao P'ei-kuo of the Hsiao Shan Temple in Wu K'ang.
   k. Yü Hung from Yü Yao.
   l. Hsia-Hou K'ai.

    m. From the northern regions, Fu Sun.

    n. Hung Chün-chü of Tan Yang.

    o. Jên Yu-ch'ang of Kao An.

    p. Ch'in Ching of Hsüan Ch'eng.

    q. Shan Tao-k'ai of Tun Huang.

    r. The Lady of Ch'en Wu of Yen Hsien.

    s. Shan Ch'ien-chih of Ho Nei.

7. In the Later Wei, Wang Su of Lan Yeh.

8. In the Sung

    a. Wang-Tzu Luan.

    b. His brother, Wang-Tzu Shang.

    c. Pao Chao and his sister, Pao Ling-hui.

9. Wu Ti, founder of the Ch'i Dynasty.

10. T'ao Hung-ching of the Liang Dynasty.

11. In the Present Dynasty, Hsü Ying-chi.

Shên Nung's *Treatise on Food* says: Tea gives one vigor of body, contentment of mind, and determination of purpose, when taken over a long period of time.

The dictionary, the *Erh Ya*, by the Duke of Chou states: The word *chia* is used to denote tea when it is bitter.

The *Kuang Ya*: In the States of Ching and Pa, the

residents pick the leaf and make cakes of it. When the leaf is old, the cake becomes firm but can be softened with an oil expressed from rice. When they are ready to brew it for drinking, they will roast it until it gets a red color to it. Then they pound and grind it and put it in a jar of stoneware. Then they steep it under cover. In addition, they will mix in onion, jujube fruit or oranges. The whole constitutes a formidable liquor that will prevent one from sleeping.

The *Yen Tzu Ch'un-Ch'iu*: When Ying [i.e., Yen Ying or Yen Tzu] served as Minister to the Duke Ching of Ch'i, he frequently took a bowl of hulled rice, five eggs, some tea and vegetables.

Ssu-Ma Hsiang-ju's "Fan Chiang" speaks of the following: Bird's beak, the balloon flower, the garland flower, colt's foot, the lily, wormwood, chickweed, peony, cinnamon, *cardus crispus,* the *fei lien,* the fungus, tea praised for its lightness, the parsnip, the cane palm, eulalia, jasmine, pepper and dogwood.

Yang Hsiung's *Fang Yen* or *Book of Dialects* tells us that in the southwestern part of Szechwan, the inhabitants use the word *shê* for tea.

From the "Biography of Wei Yao" in the *Annals of Wu*: At the banquets given by Sun Hao, Sun always counted on seven pints as the limit. Although some could not drink it all down, they surreptitiously poured it on the ground until it was gone. Yao never drank more than two pints. Hao, with an extraordinary sense of what is meet, quietly give him tea instead of wine.

The *Book of Chin*, "Chung Hsing Period": Lu Na was prefect of Wu Hsing. The General Hsieh An frequently expressed the wish to visit Na. Na's nephew, Lu Shu, blamed his uncle because no preparations had been made. Not daring to raise the question with him, he privately stored up provisions for several scores of guests. When the general arrived, all that was set out for him was tea and fruit. But suddenly Shu appeared bearing provisions and delicacies and punctiliously served them in the proper utensils. As soon as An left, Na caned Shu, giving him forty strokes and said, "You have never been able to do anything to make the life of your father's younger brother brighter or more profitable. Why then must you complicate even my simplest affairs?"

The Collected Records of the Spirits: Hsia-Hou K'ai died following an illness. One of his fellow clansmen whose name was Hsia-Hou followed him to the spirit world to investigate. He called for his horse and was about to leave when he too fell ill. His wife, donning her headpiece and outer garments, came to sit with him; when he revived, he was in his large bed by the west wall.

The first request he made was for a cup of tea.

Liu Kun wrote to his nephew Liu Yen, Governor of the southern part of Yen Chou, and said, "I have already received from An Chou one catty each of dried ginger, cassia and skullcap. They are the things I needed, but I continue sluggish and am the captive of melancholy. I seem to think of nothing but some real tea. Do you think you might arrange it?"

The Director of Criminal Justice observed that in parts of the South, distressed Szechwanese women made a sort of gruel from tea which they were able to sell for very little. He said, "I hear also that they pound it and sell the cakes in the market. How would it be if I were to restrict the sales of such things to those old women?"

The *Records of Prodigies*: Yü Hung, a man of Yü Yao, went into the mountains to gather tea and came upon a Taoist monk leading three young bullocks. Leading Hung up to the Cascade Peak, from which the water dropped straight down like a strip of calico suspended in air, he said: "I am Tan Ch'iu-tzu. I have heard it that my Master likes much to drink Tea and has for a long time hoped to visit the Hui Mountains. Deep in those mountains there are huge tea trees from which there should be enough to supply us all. May I beg of my Master that on another occasion, he will bring a tea bowl and make sacrifices to them? What is left over, I hope he will leave behind for others."

Acting upon that suggestion, he offered a libation in sacrifice. From then on there was enough for all the householders to come into the mountains and harvest the fruits of those huge trees.

Tso Ssu has a poem "Gracious Ladies."

There is a gracious lady in my home.
Her complexion is surpassing white
    dazzling white, glistening white.
She was called Wan Su — White silk
    finely spun.
Each part — the mouth, her teeth, her
    nose — is fine and true.
Her younger sister is Hui Fang: Gentle
    Fragrance
With eyes and eyebrows that are living
    paintings.

The Wild Duck soars and then hovers
    over my garden orchard.
The fruit has fallen, fresh, and
    ready to pick.
I long for flowers that bend with the
    wind and rain.
In my mind I write a play about Tea.
The wind breathes and sighs among the
    tripods and cauldrons.

"Climbing the Tower in Ch'eng Tu" by Chang
Meng-yang:

May I ask the way to Yang Tzu's hut?
I must visit the home of that great minister.
The journey is long, but I have much gold.
My horse rears and would be off for the five capitals.
At the gate, mounted guests crowd and touch.
In my turquoise sash, I carry a curving blade.
There is rice in the tripod — we go in at leisure.
The amenities are supreme perfection.
We enter the forests to pluck autumn oranges,
Visit the rivers for spring fish.
A speckled egg is finer than fine pastry.
Fruits delight more than the crab,
While fragrant Tea stills the six passions
And its encompassing flavors fill the nine provinces.
Our lives are of small account — we rest in peace.
This is a land to be savored.

In Fu Sun's *The Seven Admonishments* are mentioned many plants and trees. They include the golden peach and the crabapple; the persimmons of Ch'i and the chestnut of Yen; the yellow pear of Huan Yang; the red orange of Wu Shan; the white sugar of the extreme west and teas from the South and central regions.

Hung Chün-chü says, "When food is either supremely cold or hot, one should lie down upon having done with it. If tea, plucked after a frost, is served, one may have three cups, but he must then lie down. Among the soups no more is allowable than one cup each of those made with the mallow, olives, the five flavors; the arbutus, the plum, the quince, or with sugar cane suspended in it.

In the *Ballads* of Sun Ch'u we learn that the medicinal dogwood comes from the top of a fragrant tree; the carp comes from springs made by the River Lo; table salt, from the Ho Tung tributary of the Yellow River and soya, from Lu Yüan.

Ginger, cassia and tea are from Szechwan while peppers, oranges and magnolias come from Kao Shan.

Smartweed and thyme come from the ditches and darnel, from the fallow fields.

The *Dissertation on Foods* by Hua T'o: If bitter tea be taken over an extended period, it will quicken one's power of thought.

On the other hand, Hu Chü-shih in his *Supersti-*

tions about Foods says that if bitter tea should be taken as a practice or be eaten as leeks, obesity will follow.

Kuo P'u in his *Commentary* on the *Erh Ya*: When the tree is young, it is like a flowering gardenia. Winter leaf can be boiled into a soup and drunk. When the leaf is plucked early, it is called *ch'a*; if taken later, it is referred to as *ming* or *ch'uan*. Szechwanese call it "bitter tea."

In the *Shih shuo*, it is said of Jen Chan, otherwise known as Yu Ch'ang, a young man of good name, that on one occasion he crossed the river but found his spirit flagging. He decided to revive himself with a tea and asked some local people what kind of tea it was. Noticing looks of anger, he explained. "All I meant by the question was to ascertain if it should be drunk hot or cold."

The *Supplement to the Collected Records of the Spirits*: During the period from 265–290 of the Chin Dynasty a man named Ch'in Ching was wont to go into the mountains for tea. During one visit there, he encountered a man, covered with hair and over ten feet tall. He led Ching down the mountain, pointed to a tea tree ready for harvesting. Then he departed. But in a twinkling he reappeared, pulled an orange from his bosom and left it for Ching. Terrified, Ching seized his tea, threw it over his shoulders and was away.

During the revolt of the Four Princes in the Chin Dynasty, the Emperor Hui Ti decamped. When he returned to Lo Yang, a eunuch filled a bowl of tea and offered it to him. It was the ultimate form of honor.

From the *Anthology of Wonders*: When the Lady of Ch'en Wu was young, she was forced to live with only her two children for friends. All of them were devoted to tea.

There was, however, in the neighborhood, an old graveyard, and every time they took tea, they would have to go through the motions of making obeisance to it. The two sons grew to hate it and said, "It is an ancient graveyard. Why should we know about them and trouble ourselves so uselessly?" They thought strongly of disinterring the bodies and getting rid of the graveyard. It was an act that their mother prevented only with great difficulty.

That evening she had a dream in which a man appeared and said, "I have rested here in this old grave for over three hundred years, yet my two young lords talk incessantly of its destruction. They think they can do that and thus protect each other while they enjoy my good tea which has grown in this graveyard. Well they can easily conceal my decayed and moldering bones. But how will they avoid the retribution of mulberry trees withered and fallen?"

When morning dawned over the courtyard, the mother found over a million *cash* which she set about gathering. They looked as if they had been buried in ages past, but they were newly strung. She reported all this to her two sons who were humiliated. From that time on, they were more deeply reverential than ever.

From the *Biographies of the Elderly of Kuang Ling*: During the time of Yüan Ti of the Chin Dynasty, there was an old woman who each morning filled a vessel with tea and took it to market. Customers jostled and quarreled with one another in their rush to buy it. But although she sold from it all day long, the container remained full.

The money that the old woman received she scattered along the roadsides for orphans, poor people and beggars. Many of the people in her neighborhood began to take fright at such marvels and so the Justice in the Prefecture had her incarcerated.

That evening the old woman flew out the window of the jail on the vessel from which she sold her tea.

Shan Tao-k'ai of Tun Huang in the *Chronicles of the Arts*: Do not fear the hot or cold but take small stones regularly. The medicines taken by the Master included the essence of pine, cassia or honey. As for the rest, he took only thyme or tea.

Supplement to Tales of Buddhists and Taoists, "Accounts of Famous Monks": During the Yung Chia period of the Sung Dynasty, the Buddhist Yao from the family of Yang of Ho Tung was crossing a broad expanse of water. On his way, he met Shen T'ai-chên whom he invited to the Temple of the Small Mountain in Wu K'ang. He had already tied up his carriage, being in the twilight of his life. During the meal, tea was drunk. Once, he was invited on imperial order to make a ceremonial visit to the capital from Wu Hsing. He was then seventy-nine years old.

Family Chronicle of the Chiang, Sung Dynasty: When Chiang T'ung-shan accepted the post of groom to the heir apparent, an admonishing memorial was sent into the throne stating: "In the West Garden, we are selling sour flour, smartweed and herb tea. We presume to fear that the national honor has been stained."

The Records of the Sung: Wang-Tzu Lüan of Hsin An and Wang-Tzu Shang of Yü Chang paid a visit in the Mountain of the Eight Dukes to a Taoist from T'an Chi. After savoring the tea laid for them, one protested: "This is nothing less than sweet and peaceful dew fallen from Heaven. How can you call it tea?"

The *Poems* of Wang Wei:

> *Silently, silently I steal into my chambers.*
> *Deserted.*
> *Deserted and barren is the grand hall.*
> *Waiting.*
> *Waiting for a man who will not return.*
> *Resigned, I go to my tea.*

Pao Ling-hui, younger sister of Pao Chao, wrote a poem called "Scented Tea."

When the founder of the Southern Ch'i, the Emperor Wu, died, he left this last proclamation: "My spirit sits upon the throne. Take heed that you not sacrifice a beast, but instead lay out only cakes, fruits and tea to drink with them; dried rice, wine and dried meat."

T'ao Hung-ching in the *Records of Miscellany*: When bitter tea is too light, it should be mixed with other juices. In olden times, Tan Ch'iu-tzu, the Lord of Yellow Mountain, used it.

The Records of the Later Wei: Wang Su of Lan Yeh took office in the South. He was a lover of tea and even had his special blend. But when he returned to the North, he preferred mutton and curds to tea. Someone, wanting to know how tea compared to curds, inquired about it from him and he replied, "Tea is unworthy to be a slave to curds."

The Records of T'ung Chün: People who come from Hsi Yang, Wu Ch'ang, Lu Chiang and Hsi Ling — all from the East — love tea to a man. They make a very clear tea that, if drunk while it is still frothy, is most agreeable. It is the case with potables that most of them are manufactured from the leaves whereas such plants as asparagus are pulled up by the roots. Either way, both types of plant are very kind to man.

In the eastern part of Szechwan there is still another plant that produces genuine tea. That tea, boiled and drunk hot, will help us to stay alert.

Among the commoners, it is a usual practice to mix black plums with an infusion of sandalwood leaves. The tea made from that mixture may also be drunk cold.

Also in the South there is a kind of gourd whose leaf much resembles tea. It is exceedingly bitter and astringent. A powdered tea is made from it whose virtue lies in making it possible for one to go an entire night without sleep. Salt workers rely almost exclusively on it as their drink and serve it freely. When important guests come, the tea is first laid and then various kinds of savories are added.

The Records of K'un Yüan: In the Prefecture of Ch'en Chou, some 350 *li* from the District of Hsü P'u is the Wu I Mountain. It is said that in periods of celebration, the *Man* Tribes will collect with kindred clans and dance and sing on the mountaintop among the tea trees.

According to the *Comprehensive Map of the Empire*, one hundred forty *li* east of the District of Lin Sui, there is a stream called Tea Brook.

The Records of Wu Hsing of Shan Ch'ien: There is a Mt. Wen twenty *li* west of Wu Ch'eng from which is produced tea for the Court.

According to the *Atlas of I Ling*, tea has been produced in the mountains of Wang Chou, Nü Kuan, Ching Mên and Huang Niu.

In the *Atlas of Yung Chia*, there is a mountain called White Tea Mountain three hundred *li* east of Yung Chia. Also there is an area called Tea Slopes about two hundred *li* south of Shan Yang according to the *Atlas of Huai Yin*.

The *Atlas of Ch'a Ling* says: Ch'a Ling derives its name from the hills and valleys there that produce tea. According to the section on "Trees" in the *Pên-ts'ao*, its tea, if bitter, is called *ming* but if it has a sweet taste, it is called *ch'a*. If the bitterness is only very subtle and if it is of a cold nature, it will be harmless. Such tea is good for sores and ulcers, enhances urination and helps get rid of phlegm. If the liquor is taken exceeding hot, it will help one to sleep but little. It should be picked in the fall.

If it is bitter, it dissipates hunger and cheers the downcast. The Commentary adds: The bitter tea is picked in the spring.

In the section on "Herbs" in the *Pên-ts'ao*, it is said that bitter *t'u* is also called *ch'a* and that the names were used interchangeably.

Tea will flourish in the winter and on sand banks, along rivers, in mountains, hills and along the roadsides. Even in the coldest of winters it will not die. Pick and dry it on the third day of the third month. The Commentary adds: "One wonders if modern-day 'tea' is indicated by the text." On tea that helps keep one awake, the Commentary to the *Pên-ts'ao* states: "It is said in the *Book of Songs*, 'Who says that *t'u* is bitter? and again, '*T'u* from yellow soil is like sugar.' All of them are herbs." T'ao, however, says that bitter tea is of the tree family and is not to be counted an herb. He says that if tea is picked in the spring, it is called "bitter tea."

The Pillow Book of Cures and Prescriptions directs us for chronic ulcers to mix bitter tea and centipedes together. Roast them until there is a sweet odor and continue to cook until they disintegrate. Then pound and strain them and boil into a soup mixed with sweet herbs.

Then wash the sores and apply the decoction.

Children's Cures: If a child is preternaturally excitable and given to sudden starts, he should be given a mixture of onion beards and bitter tea.

Tea-Producing Areas

SHAN NAN

PREFECTURE	DISTRICT	AREAS OF COMPARABLE TEAS
Best Quality		
Shan Chou	Yüan An	
	I Tu	
	I Ling	
Second Quality		
Hsiang Chou	Nan Pu	
Ching Chou	Chiang Ling	
Lowest Quality		
Hêng Chou	Heng Shan	
	Ch'a Ling	
Chin Chou	Hsi Ch'eng	
	An K'ang	
Liang Chou	Chin Niu	
	Shêng Hsiang	

PREFECTURE	DISTRICT	AREAS OF COMPARABLE TEAS
Best Quality		
Kuang Chou	Kuang Shan	
Second Quality		
Department of I Yang	Chung Shan	Hsiang Chou
Shu Chou	T'ai Hu	Ching Chou
Lowest Quality		
Shou Chou	Shêng T'ang	Hêng Shan
Ch'i Chou	Huang Mei	
Huang Chou	Ma Ch'eng	Chiang Chou Liang Chou

CHÊ HSI

Best Quality		
Hu Chou	Ch'ang Ch'eng (in the Ku Chu Mountains) Sang Ju Shih Pai Ya Shan	Shou Chou Kuang Chou Hsiang Chou Ching Chou I Yang Department ment

PREFECTURE	DISTRICT	AREAS OF COMPARABLE TEAS
	An Chi	
	Wu K'ang	Chin Chou Liang Chou
Second Quality		
Chang Chou	Chün Shan	Ching Chou
	I Hsing	I Yang Department
	Shih T'ing	
	Shan Ch'üan Szu	Shu Chou
	Ch'üan Ling	
Lowest Quality		
Hsüan Chou	Hsüan Ch'eng	Hsiang Chou
	T'ai P'ing (Shang Mu and Lin Mu Mountain)	Huang Chou
Hang Chou	T'ien Mu Mountains in Lin An and Yü Ch'ien	Shu Chou
	Ch'ien T'ang (T'ien Chu and Ling Yen Monasteries)	
Mu Chou	T'ung Lu	
Hsi Chou	Wu Yüan Mountains	Hêng Chou
Jun Chou	Chiang Ning (The Ao Mountains)	

PREFECTURE	DISTRICT	AREAS OF COMPARABLE TEAS
Su Chou	Ch'ang Chou (Tung T'ing Mountain)	Liang Chou Ch'i Chou

CHIEN NAN

Best Quality

P'eng Chou	Chiu Lung (Ma An Mountains) The Monastery of Crowning Virtue P'eng Kou	Hsiang Chou

Second Quality

Mien Chou	Sung Ling Kuan Hsi Ch'ang Chang Ming Shên Ch'üan (Hsi Shan Mountain) NOTE: Teas over the Sung Ling Mountains are not worth the picking.	Ching Chou
Shu Chou	Ch'ing Ch'eng (Chang Jên Mountains)	Mien Chou

PREFECTURE	DISTRICT	AREAS OF COMPARABLE TEAS
Third Quality		
Ch'iung Chou		
Lowest Quality		
Ya Chou	Pai Chang Mountains Ming Mountains	
Lu Chou		Chin Chou
Mei Chou	Tan Hsiao (T'ieh Shan Mountains)	
Han Chou	Mien Chu (Chu Shan Mountains)	Jun Chou

CHÊ TUNG

Best Quality		
Yüeh Chou	Yü Yao (P'ao Pu Ch'üan Range) NOTE: Its tea is called "Tea of the Immortals." The large leaf is most extraordinary.	Hsiang Chou (Small leaf)

147

PREFECTURE	DISTRICT	AREAS OF COMPARABLE TEAS
Second Quality		
Ming Chou	Yü Chia Village	
Wu Chou	Tung Yang (Tung Mu Mountains)	Ching Chou
Lowest Quality		
T'ai Chou	Fêng Hsien	Hsi Chou

In Chiang Nan the tea areas are O Chou, Yüan Chou and Chi Chou.

In Chien Chung teas are produced in En Chou, Po Chou, Fu Chou and I Chou.

In Ling Nan the production areas include Fu Chou, Chien Chou, Shao Chou and Hsiang Chou. The areas in Fu Chou where tea is grown are the mountainous regions of the Min River and the District of Shan T'ao.

The eleven prefectures of En, Po, Fei, I, O, Yüan, Chi, Fu, Chien, Shao and Hsiang have not yet been extensively explored. But the flavor of the tea to be got in those areas achieves an exquisite fineness.

Generalities

CONCERNING THE PREPARATION AND UTENSILS: If it is that time of spring when there is a ban on fires and one has nevertheless plucked some tea out in the wilds, or perhaps from a Monastery or a mountain garden or coppice; and if he has already steamed, ground, roasted and dried it by fire, he may dispense with some seven steps. That is to say, he need not shave it; pound it; dry it with charcoal over a drying hole; string it, hang it in a drying shed; tie it or put it in a storage container. All those steps and the related equipment may be ignored.

Concerning the équipage for brewing tea: If among the pines, there is a rock on which one can sit, he may omit the utensil rack.

If he is using dry firewood and a tripod frame, then the brazier, cinder receptacle, stoker, fire tongs and the stand can be eliminated.

Should one be lucky enough to discover a clear spring or happen upon a fast-running stream, he need not use the water dispenser, the scouring box or the water filter.

If there are only five guests or fewer and the host selects the very quintessence of teas for tasting, he may dispense with the netting to strain the tea.

Further if one is trying to escape the brambles; if he is scrambling up a steep cliff; or if he is faced with pulling himself by a rope ladder up into a mountain cave to heat and grind his tea, he may pass over the roller, brush and grinder — provided he stores it in a paper bag or casket.

It is even permissible not to use the carryall if a fruit basket will answer for carrying the rest of the équipage, viz., the gourd ladle, the bowls, the chopsticks, writing equipment, cooking implements, cups and salt containers.

However, when in the walled city at the gate of a Prince or Duke, if the Twenty-Four Implements find their number diminished by only one, then it is best to dispense with the tea.

Plan of the Book

O N WHITE SILK OF FOUR OR SIX ROLLS, copy it so that it can be hung in sections. Spread the sections out in order in the corner of the room where the seats would be. Arrange them so that "The Beginnings of Tea," "The Tools of Tea," "The Manufacture of Tea," "The Équipage," "The Brewing of Tea," "Drinking the Tea," "Notations on Tea," "Tea-Producing Areas" and "Generalities" can be taken in at a glance and retained in memory.

With that, from first to last will have been completed this treatise on tea.

NOTES

THE TEXT TO WHICH THE NOTES REFER is indicated below by page and paragraph, the number of the page followed by the *final word* of the paragraph. When a paragraph carries over from one page to another, the number of the second page is given.

11 *people:* See note for page 116 for more details on Shên Nung.
13 *context:* Sow-thistle's scientific name is *Sonchus* and flowering rush would be *Euryale.*
13 *earlier:* Shepherd's purse is *Bursa pastoris.*
13 *China:* See Section 10, p. 26b.
16 *headache:* Tea may have been second only to ginseng in the number of recipes in which it figures even in early China. Extracting the *Pên-ts'ao kang-mu,* DuHalde cites a score or more complaints for which tea is the drug of choice. One example is a "Receipt for a Noise in the Head: Take white Ants of the largest sort dry'd, with some Seed of Tea, reduce them to a Powder and blow them up the Nostrils. This Remedy has a good Effect" (P. J. B. DuHalde, *A Description of the Empire of China and*

Chinese-Tartary, Together with the Kingdoms of Korea and Tibet, London, 1741, Vol. II, p. 224).

17 *paintings:* See Okakura-Kakuzo, *The Book of Tea,* New York, 1906, p. 26.

22 *sings:* The term *pai-hao* eventually made its way into the western language as "Pekoe."

29 *catty:* See Williams, S. Wells, "Description of the Tea Plant," *The Chinese Repository,* Vol. VIII, No. 3, 1839, pp. 132–164.

29 *équipage:* The T'ien-Mu Mountains are in Chekiang Province whereas the "humble wares of Chien," to borrow a phrase from Professor James M. Plummer, were actually made in Fukien Province. It would appear that they were first called *Temmoku* by the Japanese, whose visiting monks must have seen them at a monastery in the T'ien-Mu Mountains.

30 *leaves:* Ching-tê Chen is the site of the very famous kilns in Kiangsi Province. It is located at 29°18'–117°12'.

30 *leaves:* Chiang Nan in Ming times comprised Anhui and Kiangsu provinces.

31 *powers:* Wu I got its name from two brothers, whose given names were Wu and I. They seem to have discovered tea there, and, leaving their own patrimony, came to the hills to live. Wu I tea was to become known as Bohea in the West. Because the tea *imported* from there was inexpensive and of a lower grade, it is frequently spoken of as "lowly Bohea."

34 *guests:* Although an agreement had been reached in 1494 between Spain and Portugal that gave Portugal rights to the world east of a north-south line through the Cape Verde Islands, the Spanish argued that since they had sailed west across the Pacific, they were holding to their part of the pact.

35 *Empire:* See Reinaud, *Relations des Voyages fait par les Arabes et les Persans dans l'Inde et à la Chine,* I, 1845, p. 40.

36 *rhubarb:* It seems to have been a deep-rooted conviction with many Chinese that rhubarb was a necessity of consummate importance to Europeans, who would die if the Chinese ceased to supply the plant.

37 *1615:* Along with those mentioned in the text, there was a spate of references to tea in the early seventeenth century as more and more people went to China and found the courage to taste it. The

judgment is almost universally favorable. In a century when health was an absorbing concern, tea's medicinal properties were accorded serious and positive attention. Tabulated below are the most important seventeenth-century references to the drink.

1. Father Gaspar da Crux gave an early account in Portuguese and is quoted in Samuel Purchas, *Purchas His Pilgrimes,* London, 1625.

2. Doctor Jacob Bontius, a Dutch resident of Batavia, gives a short notice of tea in his 1631 edition of *Historia naturalis et med. Indiae orientalis.*

3. In 1638, Ambassador Starkoff refused a gift of tea for the tzar feeling that His Highness would find no use for it.

4. Father Alvaro Semedo, a Portuguese, is the first of the missionaries to give an account of the plant, its botanical character and the preparation of the drink. Though he wrote his account of China, *Relatione della Grande Monarchia della Cina,* in 1633, it was not published in Rome until a decade later. He mentions also that it is an honor to be offered tea, but when it is offered for the third time, it is a signal for the guest to take leave.

5. In 1648, tea made its appearance in Paris where it was indeed "abused as its popularity spread," for it was born there under the stigma of Dr. Guy Patin's characterization as the "impertinente nouveauté du siècle."

6. Martinus Martini gives a good account of the tea plant, its cultivation and its preparation in the *Novus Atlas Sinensis,* 1655 (p. 106).

7. The Dutch Jan Nieuhoff, whose book *An Embassy from the East India Company of the United Provinces to the Grand Tartar Cham, Emperor of China* was translated into English in 1673, said of tea: "But amongst all others, China is famous for an Herb called Thea or Cha . . . and that this is a sort of Sumack none need to doubt; however, it springs not wild, but by manuring, is no Tree . . . but a Bush which they plant upon little Hills three feet asunder, and grow as high as a Rose-tree."

37 *China:* See especially Volume I, beginning page 368, for a discussion of the plant.

40 *departure:* There was very little that Linnaeus wrote about Chinese plants that he did not learn from Osbek, who collected 244 new plants. Linnaeus's ignorance of East Asian geography seems to have been profound. For example, he named the rose *Rosa indica* because he thought Canton, where it was gathered, was in India rather than China.

41 *Chusan:* See Petiver, James, *Musei Petiveriani Centuriae Decem Rariora Naturae Continens,* items 984 and 985; Petiver, *Gazophylacium Naturae et artis;* see also Plukenet, Leonard, *Amaltheum botanicum,* where he describes the *Thea viridis* (green tea. There is, of course, no such plant).

45 *proceed:* Coordinates for the places named are as follows: Hsing Ts'un: 27°39′–117°52′; Ho K'ou: 28°16′–117°37′; Kan Chou: 25°52′–114°54′; Ta Yü: 20°30′–114°19′.

46 *West:* Shih Hsing is located at 25°02′–114°03′ and Chiu Chiang at 22°49′–113°02′.

51 *hemp:* Ching Ling is presently known as T'ien Men ("Gate of Heaven") and is located at 30°39′–113°15′.

52 *Lu Yü:* The flower *Lu T'iao* is the *Tecoma grandiflora.*

52 *original:* The two compendia were *An Anthology of T'ang and Sung Writers* where it was item forty-seven and *A Collection of One Hundred Famous Writers* (there were actually ninety-eight in the collection) where it was item seventy-five.

59 *walnut:* Gardenia = *Gardenia florida.*

61 *all:* Ladybell = *Adenophora remotiflora.*

61 *all:* Heaven produces six vapors or atmospheric influences which in turn descend to create the five flavors (salt, bitter, sour, acid, sweet); the five sounds or the five notes of the ancient pentatonic scale (*kung, shang, chiao, chih, yü*) and the five colors which are red, black, greenish-blue, white and yellow. When any of these are out of harmony, one of the six illnesses can arise because of too much of one or the other of the six atmospheric influences. The atmospheric influences are *yin* (the female principle) and *yang* (the male principle), wind, rain, darkness and brightness, which are in turn governed by the five elements of earth, water, wood, metal and fire. An excess of vapors creates an illness as:
1. An excess of *yin* creates chills.
2. An excess of *yang* creates fever.

3. An excess of wind creates illness of the four limbs.
4. An excess of rain creates illness of the stomach.
5. An excess of darkness leads to delusions.
6. An excess of light creates illness in the heart.

65 *ornamented:* We must bear in mind that during T'ang times, the normal way to manufacture tea was in bricks. Loose tea did not come into common usage until the period of the Sung dynasty (tenth to thirteenth centuries).

65 *process:* Pagoda tree = *Sophora japonica.*

66 *tea:* Measures of length, capacity and weight have for the sake of convenience been translated into terms familiar to western readers. The three measures of length used by Lu Yü include the *fên,* the *ts'un,* the *chih.* Ten *fên* = one *ts'un* and ten *ts'un* = one *chih.* Ten *chih* = one *chang.* Although the measures of length varied in value from age to age, consistency within a period is a mark of the strength of the reign. The *chih's* value seems to have been quite stable in Lu Yü's time, being about 12.6 inches. By the time the West was involved with China, the value was 14.1 inches.

The important units of capacity are the *ho,* ten of which make a *shêng* (roughly equivalent to a pint). Ten *shêng* = a *tou,* translated here as a gallon.

69 *smallest:* The area Lu speaks of comprises the present-day provinces of Kiangsu and Anhui.

69 *smallest:* Chinese weights include some that are only nominal. The most important were the *liang,* somewhat equivalent to our ounce; the *chin* or catty, containing sixteen *liang,* and therefore roughly equivalent to our pound; the *tan* of 100 *chin.*

Weights, like other measures, varied in value in different parts of the country but tended to shrink in value the nearer they got to the capital. They varied in value by time period as well. During the time of Lu Yü, the value of the *chin* or catty was probably a bit more than 19 ounces.

69 *fire:* Chiang Nan was one of ten, later fifteen, subdivisions of China in the T'ang dynasty called "tao." See reference for page 148 (Chi Chou).

70 *cool:* In T'ang times, a lunar calendar was universally used, hence the translation *moon* in preference to *month.*

72 *frost:* The seven steps alluded to are picking, steaming, pounding, shaping, drying, tying and sealing.

77 *illnesses:* The text says, "On it" rather than "On mine." However, it becomes clear that he is talking about his own.

77 *illnesses:* K'an, Sun and Li are three of the eight trigrams on which the philosophy of the *I Ching* or *Book of Changes* is based. The trigrams consist of various combinations of a solid line representing the force of *yang* (the male principle) and a broken one representing the force of *yin* (the female principle). Charged with great meaning for the Chinese, the trigrams and their derivatives, the hexagrams, pictured, embodied and helped to shape the lives of the Chinese.

Lu explains *why* these particular three trigrams are on his brazier. To describe them:

$$k'an = \overline{}\ \overline{};\quad sun = \overline{};\quad li = \overline{}\ \overline{}$$

K'an is the Abysmal whose image is *Water*. He signifies danger, and his color is red. He is the moon, due north, midwinter and midnight.

Sun is the Gentle whose image is *wind*. She signifies vegetative power. Her color is white and she is the southeast and forenoon.

Li has a *fire* image. She occupies the south, her time is summer and midday. For more detail, see Hellmut Wilhelm, *Change — Eight Lectures on the I Ching,* New York, 1960.

77 *illnesses:* The five elements are fire, earth, water, wood, metal.

77 *illnesses:* The hundred illnesses are defined by one commentator as troubles arising from disruption and deceit.

81 *fu:* Hammer or ax.

82 *unadulterated:* Tossing tea was an art and an arduous one. The worker, to keep the tea from burning, had to dip his hands into a red-hot pan and keep the loose tea circulating. He became inured to the heat after many years of almost continuous practice of the art.

85 *feathers: t'ung = Paulownia tomentosa.*

85 *feathers: Chê* is a Chinese tree of a very hard wood. The *Pên-ts'ao kang-mu,* a Chinese herbal, says of it, "It is found everywhere in the mountains and likes to grow in thickets. It grows tall

and straight and its leaves are succulent and thick. Its leaves are used to feed silkworms, and its fruit is like that of the mulberry though as round as a peppercorn. The tree also produces a dye of a yellowish-reddish color called *chê* yellow."

86 *inches:* The precise kind of tree Lu has in mind for *shan* may not be clear except that it is an evergreen, perhaps *Cunninghamia sinensis* or *Cryptomeria japonica.*

86 *more:* See note for page 66 (tea) on measures of capacity.

87 *pints:* The *chou* tree seems at one time to have covered much of China, but may be now extinct. It is apparently an evergreen, for the *Shan Hai Ching,* one of China's early classics, says of it that even in the bitter cold the leaves will not fall.

87 *pints:* Respectively after the *chou* tree, the trees enumerated are the *Sophora japonica, Mallotus japonicus* and either *Catalpa ovata* or *Catalpa kaempferi.*

89 *wood:* A *fu* is a kind of prose poem or verse narration.

89 *wood:* The Yung Chia period was about A.D. 307. It is the period of the Chin dynasty. Lu draws much on that period for his records of tea.

89 *wood:* Yü Yao is in modern Chekiang Province.

90 *Salt Dish:* Pronounced *kuei,* the character originally signified a bamboo basket used for holding grain at a sacrifice.

90 *Chou:* Yüeh Chou ware represents one of the oldest examples of China's long and proud ceramic tradition. It appears to have been made as early as the Han dynasty, and has a gray-green glaze that could have been the first of the so-called celadons. While it has such a long history, its kiln site was not discovered until 1930. The site was discovered by Yanaiyama near Yü Yao. From the third century A.D. through T'ang times, it was produced in large quantities. Lu Yü was no doubt best acquainted with that type of ware.

90 *Chou:* Ting ware became most popular perhaps during the Northern Sung period (late tenth through early twelfth centuries). At that time almost the entire production of the Ting kilns was a pure white with either molded or incised designs and with copper rims. Some of the work was of eggshell thickness. It is extremely interesting to note its popularity in the mid-eighth century. One even wonders if Lu was referring to white or red

Ting, and it is particularly tempting to wonder if he might not have been talking about the fabled Ju ware reputed to have been a product of the Ting Chou kilns. It is Ju ware whose glaze has been described by an imaginative writer as the blue of the sky as it appears through a rift in the clouds after a rainstorm.

90 *Chou:* The second notice of Yüeh Chou is for a different place from the one discussed in the note above.

92 *bowls:* Hsing Chou ware originated in kilns in Hupei Province near Nei Ch'iu in a place called Hsing Tai. It is said to have been "as white and soft as snow." It seems to have begun in T'ang times and no doubt was appealing to those who wanted the latest thing and was somewhat repugnant to men such as Lu who inclined to wares crusty with tradition.

92 *bowls:* The metaphors concerning Yüeh Chou and Hsing Chou both give the nod to Yüeh Chou ware as slightly better, but at the same time allude to characteristics of the wares. Hence "ice" may well suggest a crackle in Yüeh bowls while "snow" suggests the color of the others.

92 *bowls:* Tu Yü was a man of letters, a famous commentator and a military expert. His life spanned most of the third century A.D. He had an absorbing passion for the classics and once described himself as having a sickness for the Tso Ch'iu-ming commentary on the *Ch'un-ch'iu.* At the same time, he subdued so many of the armies from the state of Wu that he became known as Tu Chêng-nan, the Subjugator of the South.

94 *brush:* Coir palm = *Trachycarpus excelsa.*

94 *brush:* Dogwood = *Cornus officinalis.*

105 *fuel:* The commentary adds: "The best of pulverized tea is like the fine chaff of threshed rice. The inferior kind is like the water chestnut."

105 *fuel:* The fuel Lu has in mind is either mulberry, the pagoda tree, the *t'ung,* or oak (*Quercus serrata*).

105 *fuel:* The oily woods included cedar, cassia and juniper.

105 *Min:* The Min here referred to is in Szechwan.

107 *out:* To say the dragon may be sequestered is to say the water has lost its virtue. The dragon is an auspicious creature and his disappearance, especially from water (which he represents — as he does spring and all that is green), would be a bad omen.

113 *ch'a:* Another text says, "When the flavor is bitter and not sweet, it is *chia*. When it is sweet and not bitter, it is *ch'uan*."

116 *tea:* Shên Nung is one of the most famous of the mythical figures. His name is commonly translated as the Divine Husbandman, and he is said to have ruled around 2737 B.C. Mayer tells us that his mother conceived under the influence of a heavenly dragon. He is supposed to have reigned under the influence of the fire element and so is called Yen Ti, the Fire Emperor. He taught people husbandry, invented the plough and discovered the curative value of plants. He is almost inevitably the choice for the discoverer of tea.

116 *tea:* Almost as famous as Shên Nung is the Duke of Chou, who is an only slightly more authentic historical figure. A man of the twelfth century B.C., he is represented as the paragon of all those values and virtues which the Chinese hold to be good. He drew up the ordinances of the empire, says Mayer, directed its policy and purified its morals. The State of Lu, his fiefdom, was also to be the birthplace of Confucius. It is interesting that the Duke of Chou seems also to have been a familiar spirit of Confucius appearing to him in dreams from time to time.

116 *tea:* Yen Ying flourished during the fifth century B.C. and is, like the Duke of Chou, considered a paragon among statesmen.

116 *tea:* Both Yang Hsiung and Ssu-Ma Hsiang-ju were famous scholars, philosophers and administrators although Yang's reputation is somewhat more maculate for having accepted a position under the usurping Emperor Wang Mang.

120 *Period of the Three Emperors (item 1):* The Three Emperors included Fu Hsi, Huang Ti and Shên Nung. Fu Hsi was the founder of China, having descended from the Divines who ruled long before human society was constituted. As with the other legendary rulers, his was a miraculous birth, his mother having conceived by the influence of Heaven and then having endured a pregnancy that lasted twelve years. He taught the people to cook, deciphered the Chinese writing system, established the seasons and invented musical instruments.

Huang Ti, or the Yellow Emperor, was born in the first half of the third millennium B.C. again by a miraculous conception. Since he reigned under the influence of the Earth element, he obtained the sobriquet of Huang or Yellow. He taught the people to make utensils of wood, pottery and metal. He succeeded in developing medical practice to prolong life and died himself at the age of 111. It was his consort who taught the people to weave silk and grow silkworms.

120 *Chou Dynasty (item 2):* The dynasties with which Lu Yü is concerned have the following approximate dates:

1. The Legendary Period — third millennium B.C.
2. The Hsia dynasty — second millennium B.C.
3. The Shang dynasty — perhaps eighteenth century B.C. to twelfth century B.C.
4. Chou — twelfth to third century B.C.
5. Ch'in — 221 B.C. to 206 B.C.
6. Han — 206 B.C. to A.D. 221
7. The Period of the Three Kingdoms
   a. The Shu Han dynasty — 221–263
   b. The Wei dynasty — 220–265
   c. The Wu dynasty — 222–277
8. The Chin dynasty
   a. The Western Chin — 265–317
   b. The Eastern Chin — 317–420
9. The Division between North and South
   A. The Southern dynasties
      a. The Liu Sung — 420–479
      b. The Ch'i — 479–502
      c. The Liang — 502–557
      d. The Ch'en — 557–587
   B. The Northern dynasties
      a. The Northern Wei — 386–535
      b. The Western Wei — 535–554
      c. The Eastern Wei — 534–550
      d. The Northern Ch'i — 550–557
      e. The Northern Chou — 557–581
10. The Sui dynasty — 589–618
11. The T'ang dynasty — 618–906

120 *Item 4b:* Ssu-Ma Hsiang-ju was a famous poet, scholar and lover who was forced to run away to escape an angry father. He made his way back to fame during the period of Han Wu-ti and died

about 117 B.C. Ssu-Ma is one of the common double surnames.

120 *Item 5:* A.D. 264–277.

121 *Item 6:* There was a Western Chin which lasted fifty-two years from 265–317 and an Eastern Chin from 317–420. The period seems to be the one to which Lu Yü most commonly refers. It would suggest that either Lu was much concerned with the Chin or that tea had taken a firm place by that time in the life of the Chinese (or both).

121 *Item 6a:* A.D. 290–307.

121 Item *6i:* Tu Yü has already been quoted from his *Poem on Tea* several times.

122 *Item 8:* That is, the Liu Sung, A.D. 420–479. All references to the Sung will be to the Liu Sung.

122 *Item 8a:* Wang-Tzu is another double surname.

122 *bitter:* Whether or not the *Erh Ya* in the state available to Lu Yü contained the definition is problematical. It may have been added by the fourth-century commentator on the work, Kuo P'u.

123 *sleeping:* Ching and Pa covered territory that constitutes much of present-day China, including the territory south of the Yangtze and westward to Szechwan.

123 *dogwood:* Bird's beak is a literal translation. The English equivalent may not be clear. More precise equivalents after "bird's beak" are *Platycodon grandiflorus; Daphne genkwa; Petasites japonicus, Fritillaria verticillata* var. *Thunbergii; Artemisia; Cerastium vulgatum* var. *glandulosum; Paeonia albiflora* var. *hortensis; Cinnamomum cassia; Cardus crispus; Fei lien* (see following note); *Fungus; Thea sinensis; Heracleum lanatum; Calamus; Miscanthus sinensis; Tabernae montani; Cornus officinalis.*

123 *dogwood:* While *fei lien* may be another plant, Ssu-Ma Hsiang-ju himself in a commentary says it is an animal with a bird's body and the head of a deer.

125 *wine:* Sun Hao was the Lord of Wu during the Period of the Three Kingdoms in the third century A.D. It was he who presided over the destruction of Wu by the Chin. His penchant for wine was only one of many appetites, apparently, as when he surrendered to the Chin he lost thousands of concubines.

125 *wine:* Presumably "seven pints" means seven pints of wine.

125 *affairs:* The Chung Hsing period was about 386. The reader will recall that Lu Yü speaks earlier of Lu Na as a distant ancestor.

126 *wall: The Collected Records of the Spirits* was edited by Kan Pao of the Chin dynasty.

126 *wall:* Hsia-Hou is a double surname.

126 *it:* Skullcap = *Scutellaria baikalensis.*

127 *others:* A Han dynasty work, *Records of Prodigies* was annotated in the third century by Chang Hua of the Chin.

127 *others:* The Hui Mountains are near Wu Hsi in Kiangsu Province. They are so named because the monk, Hui Chao, dwelt in them but also they are known as the Mountain of the Spirit of the West and as Nine Dragons Mountain. They are said to have nine peaks and nine torrents. There is also a spring in the mountain called Mt. Hui Spring. Its water was particularly esteemed by Lu Yü for making tea.

127 *Ladies:* Tso Ssu was a poet of the third century during the Chin dynasty. It has been said of him that though he was plain of face and stammered in speech, the elegance of his words made him strong and beautiful.

130 *savored:* The five capitals differed at different times. In Lu Yü's time, they would have been, after Ch'ang An as the principal capital, Lo Yang in the Central area, Fêng Hsiang in the West, Chiang Ling in the South and T'ai Yüan in the North.

130 *savored:* Like the five capitals, the six passions differed with the times. One set includes pleasure, anger, grief, happiness, love and hate. Another set comprises purity, generosity and uprightness as the good passions and corruptness, villainy and meanness as the evil ones. In Buddhist terms, they are the eyes, ears, nose, tongue, body and the will (hence: form, sound, scent, taste, sensation, perception).

131 *it:* The Chinese five flavors are salt, bitter, sour, acid and sweet. Presumably five-flavor soup in the third century was a highly seasoned one.

131 *Yüan:* Sun Ch'u was something of a speechifier, says Wieger, of the Chin dynasty. He died in A.D. 285.

131 *thought:* Hua T'o was a celebrated physician, known for his legendary cures, diagnostic apparatus and for his acupuncture. He died in 220 and is a sort of God of Medicine.

132 *tea:* Kuo P'u was a famous commentator. Also a Taoist, supposed to have been acquainted with all the mysteries of alchemy and sublimation, he was one of the greatest of early authorities on antiquarianism and mysticism. He lived from 276 to 324 A.D.

132 *tea:* The *Erh Ya* is probably the first of the Chinese dictionaries about objects. It dates from a fairly early period, possibly the sixth century B.C. although attributions have been made to the Duke of Chou as its author, which would have put it in the twelfth century B.C. Kuo P'u was probably the first commentator, but during the Ch'ing dynasty many eighteenth-century scholars were attracted to it.

133 *away:* The *Supplement* was written in the fifth century during the Liu Sung dynasty. The original collection of legends was written by Kan Pao during the Chin dynasty around 320.

133 *honor:* The Hui Ti Emperor ruled from A.D. 290–306.

133 *tea:* The *I Yüan*, a collection of wondrous happenings, was written by Liu Ching-shu of the Liu Sung.

134 *full:* Yüan Ti's time was about A.D. 315.

135 *or tea:* It may not be clear, but some such practice does appear to have been a part of medical prescriptions at the time under consideration.

135 *old:* "To tie up one's carriage" is an expression indicating one does not plan to go out again, hence used of an official arriving at his post, or for twilight. By extension, then, it is used metaphorically for an old man.

136 *Wang Wei:* This particular Wang Wei was also a painter and flourished in the latter part of the fifth century.

138 *Scented Tea:* Pao Chao was a celebrated poet of the mid-fifth century. He was killed in 466.

138 *Scented Tea:* Tea was scented by placing layers of flowers between layers of tea. After it was heated, the flowers could be sifted out. The poem places the practice much earlier than has commonly been thought. The flowers most used for scenting tea included:

1. Rose
2. Plum
3. Jasmine

a. *Jasminum sambac*
b. *Jasminum paniculatum*
4. *Aglaia odorata* (also used for incense after having been filtered from tea)
5. Orange
6. Gardenia

For most of the above, the ratio was about 40 pounds of flowers to 100 pounds of tea.

138 *meat:* The Emperor Wu died in 492.

138 *it:* T'ao Hung-ching was a scholar, a mathematician, a physician and a famous Taoist. He flourished during the Liang dynasty, and he completed the material in the *Pên-ts'ao.*

138 *curds:* Wang Su was a fifth- and sixth-century general who ended his life in 501 fighting for the Northern Wei. See next note.

138 *curds:* Wang Su's preference for a "northern" drink over the "southern" tea is evidently a political one. When the southern Ch'i killed his father, he defected to the northern Wei and then fought the South. His insults to tea were very much a case of "beating the servant to hurt the concubine." The term "a slave to curds" has come to be a metaphor for tea. The "curds" may have been koumiss, a drink of fermented mare's milk.

139 *man:* T'ung Chün is a man for whom the modern T'ung Lu District in Chekiang Province is named. It seems to have acquired that name after he had taken a drug to help him find the *tao* and was himself found huddled beneath a *t'ung* tree. When asked his name, he simply pointed to the tree and people called him Mr. T'ung. Thus the district, a mountain peak, a mountain range, a river and a stream nearby are all called T'ung.

139 *alert:* The remark suggests that even in the sixth century, the Chinese were using plants other than *Thea sinensis* as tea substitutes. The following paragraphs are suggestive of things to come when in the American War of Independence, patriotic women used raspberry leaves, camomile, loosestrife and sage rather than buy the leaf from the British. Some of the plants serving as substitutes in China and to which Lu Yü is no doubt alluding include:

1. Several kinds of crabapple and wild pear including the *Malus theifera*.
2. Several species of *Spiraea* (*S. Henryi, S. Blumei, S. chinensis, S. hirsuta*).
3. Weeping willow (*Salix babylonica*).
4. *Viburnum theiferum.*

140 *trees:* K'un is one of the eight trigrams and stands for the mother, Earth. K'un Yüan indicates areas of extreme fertility able to produce all things.

140 *trees:* A *li* is approximately one-third of a mile.

141 *fall:* Ch'a Ling could be translated as Tea Hills.

141 *fall:* The *Pên-ts'ao* was a Chinese herbal attributed to the legendary Emperor Shên Nung. It has not, however, appeared in the literature until around A.D. 4 when the emperor ordered all familiar with the *Pên-ts'ao* to assemble in the capital. Li Shih-ch'i of the T'ang dynasty says it was committed to writing in the Han. In its present form, it is as quoted in the *Pên-ts'ao kang-mu,* a sixteenth-century work (of which the earliest extant edition is 1658). It includes sixteen divisions, with 62 classes, 1,892 species and 8,160 prescriptions.

141 *fall:* Concerning the "cold nature," medicines, and indeed most objects, were thought to have different natures, hot or cold, which dictated the method, type and timing of usage.

141 *fall:* Should we be inclined to scoff a bit at some of this sixth-century fancy, let us look at an *eighteenth*-century view of tea in the West:

> In Pleuritick or Peripneumonick Disorders, or Pains in the Sides, from a Distention of Pulmonary or Pleuritick Vessels with a fizy Blood, such as [one] cannot down with Linneseed, *Tea* may find a proper Succedaneum in this, seeing it dilutes and attenuates the Blood and softens the rigid Vessels, so as the gross Particles may pass. This is One of the chief Uses of Bohea Tea to which I might add its Fitness in Ulcers and Abscesses of the Reins and Bladder, where stimulating Medicines are improper, and only Lubricators fit.

169

142 *called "bitter tea":* The rest of the statement after "Who says
that *t'u* is bitter?" reads: "It is as sweet as the Shepherd's
Purse."

142 *called "bitter tea":* T'ao refers to T'ao Hung-ching, the commentator. See note for page 138 (it).

143 *Areas:* Rather than give separate notes to each place, it has
seemed best to give the location of places mentioned in one note.
Any additional useful information will be given in subsequent
notes. The locations are in the order of appearance in the text.
Places no longer identifiable have been omitted. Identifications go
no lower than the *chou* (prefectural) level.

NAME	ESTABLISHING DYNASTY	MODERN PROVINCE	PRESENT NAME	COORDINATES
Shan Chou		Hupei		
Hsiang Chou		Hupei	Hsiang Yang	32° 01′ 112° 04′
Ching Chou		Hupei	Ching Chou	30° 18′ 112° 13′
Hêng Chou	Sui	Hunan	Abolished	26° 56′ 112° 35′
Chin Chou	Western Wei	Shensi	An K'ang	32° 41′ 109° 10′
Liang Chou	Three King-doms	Shensi	Nan Chêng	32° 05′ 107° 04′
Kuang Chou	Liang	Honan	Huang Ch'uan	32° 12′ 115° 09′
I Yang	Three King-doms (Wei)	Honan	T'ung Pai	32° 22′ 113° 27′
Shu Chou		Anhui	Shu Ch'eng (?)	31° 27′ 117° 01′
Shou Chou	Sui	Anhui	Shou Hsien	32° 35′ 116° 50′
Ch'i Chou	N. Chou	Hupei	Ch'i Ch'un	30° 01′ 115° 22′
Huang Chou	Sui	Hupei	Abolished	30° 26′ 114° 52′
Hu Chou	Sui	Chekiang	Abolished	30° 53′ 120° 06′
Ch'ang Chou	Sui	Kiangsu	Abolished	31° 46′ 119° 58′
Hsüan Chou	Chin	Anhui	Hsüan Ch'eng	30° 56′ 118° 43′
Hang Chou	Sui	Chekiang	Hang Hsien	30° 17′ 120° 10′
Mu Chou	Sui	Chekiang	Ch'un An	29° 37′ 118° 57′
Hsi Chou	T'ang	Anhui	Hsi Hsien	29° 52′ 118° 26′
Jun Chou	Sui	Kiangsu	Chên Chiang	32° 12′ 119° 28′
Su Chou	Sui	Kiangsu	Abolished	31° 19′ 120° 37′
P'eng Chou	T'ang	Szechwan	P'eng Hsien	30° 59′ 103° 56′
Mien Chou	Sui	Szechwan	Mien Yang	31° 29′ 104° 46′
Shu Chou		Szechwan		
Ch'iung Chou	Liang[1]	Szechwan	Ch'iung Lai	30° 25′ 103° 29′

NAME	ESTABLISHING DYNASTY	MODERN PROVINCE	PRESENT NAME	COORDINATES
Ya Chou	Sui	Szechwan	Abolished	30° 00' 103° 02'
Lu Chou	Liang	Szechwan	Lu Hsien	28° 53' 105° 23'
Mei Chou	Later Wei	Szechwan	Mei Shan	30° 03' 103° 51'
Han Chou	T'ang	Szechwan	Kuang Han	30° 59' 104° 17'
Yüeh Chou	Sui[2]	Chekiang	Shao Hsing	30° 00' 120° 34'
Ming Chou	T'ang	Chekiang	Yin Hsien	29° 54' 121° 32'
Wu Chou	Sui	Chekiang	Chin Hua	29° 07' 119° 39'
T'ai Chou	T'ang	Chekiang	Abolished	28° 53' 121° 07'
O Chou	Sui[3]	Hupei	Wu Ch'ang	30° 32' 114° 17'
En Chou	T'ang (?)			
Po Chou	T'ang	Kueichou	Tsun I	27° 42' 106° 55'
Fei Chou	T'ang (?)			
I Chou	T'ang (?)			
Yüan Chou	Sui	Kiangsu	Abolished	27° 46' 114° 22'
Chi Chou	Sui	Kiangsi	Chi An	27° 06' 115° 00'
Fu Chou	T'ang	Fukien	Min Hou (Foochow)	26° 05' 119° 19'
Chien Chou	T'ang	Fukien	Chien Ou	27° 04' 118° 19'
Shao Chou	Sui[4]	Kwangtung	Abolished	24° 50' 113° 33'
Hsiang Chou	Sui	Kwangsi	Hsiang Hsien	24° 00' 109° 36'

1. Abolished by the T'ang but later revived.
2. Abolished in Sung.
3. Changed during Sui to Chiang Hsia but revived in T'ang dynasty.
4. Changed and then revived in T'ang dynasty.

143 *Shan Nan:* Shan Nan in T'ang times was one of ten, later fifteen, *tao*s or political subdivisions somewhat like today's province. Shan Nan was defined as being south of the Chung Nan Mountains and the T'ai Hua Mountains. It included parts or all of Hupei, Shensi, Honan and Szechwan.

144 *Huai Nan:* Huai Nan was also a T'ang *tao*. It was defined as being north of the Yangtze and south of the Huai Mountains. It included parts of Hupei, Anhui and Kiangsu provinces.

144 *Chê Hsi:* Chê Hsi was a T'ang *tao* and included the western part of Chekiang Province. It covered parts of the neighboring provinces west of Chekiang as well, i.e., Anhui and Kiangsi.

146 *Chien Nan:* Chien Nan was a T'ang *tao* and included parts of Szechwan, Kansu and Yunnan.

147 *Chê Tung:* Chê Tung was a *tao* including the area of south-eastern Chekiang Province.

148 *Chi Chou:* The *tao* of Chiang Nan, quite different from the Chiang Nan of Ming times, may have been the largest of the T'ang *taos.* It stretched across the central part of China and included parts of the modern provinces of Chekiang, Fukien, Kiangsi, Anhui, Szechwan and Kueichou. During the K'ai Yüan reign (713–742), it was divided into Chiang Nan East, Chiang Nan West and Chien Chung.

148 *I Chou:* Created as a *tao* in the K'ai Yüan (713–742) reign, Chien Chung included Hupei, Hunan, Szechwan and Kueichou or parts thereof.

148 *T'ao:* The Ling Nan area was a *tao* including the two Kuangs (Kwangtung and Kwangsi) and Annam.

148 *fineness:* Some of the eleven "unexplored" prefectures were, by the time of the West's introduction to tea, producing some of China's superlative teas. That Lu Yü scarcely knew them is a persuasive reminder of the antiquity of tea-drinking practices in China.

149 *ignored:* The ban on fire began the day before Ch'ing Ming, the Festival of Purity and Brightness. It is a celebration for the dead and has, not uncharacteristically, procreative overtones to it. All the fires were allowed to go out in order that they might be re-kindled. The notion is an organic part of Chinese philosophy that there is a proper time to rest from which one gains a new surge of energy.

During Ch'ing Ming, which occurs 106 days after the winter solstice, the dead are honored, graves decorated (with willow) and offerings made to ancestors.

TRANSLATOR'S
ACKNOWLEDGMENTS
AND NOTES

Not many people have participated in this project to produce a western-language version of the first treatise on tea. However, those who did involve themselves have helped so enormously that it is only a slight exaggeration to say that the virtues of the book are all theirs, its faults, my own.

My very warm thanks go to Mr. J. Randall Williams III and to Mr. Llewellyn Howland III for their support, encouragement and good counsel.

A very special and grateful acknowledgment is due to Demi Hitz for preparing a set of illustrations as lovely as herself. I must also acknowledge with appreciation the incorrigible optimism of Demi Hitz's father, William Morris Hunt, whose enthusiasm for the arts has no visible bounds and who has been a genuine source of encouragement in this project.

I thank almost the entire staff of the Massachusetts Horticultural Society for their support and help. I am especially thankful to Mr. Carlton B. Lees, Mrs. Muriel Crossman and Mrs. Frances C. Dowd for permitting use of their paintings and for their generous bibliographic assistance.

For their patience, good humor and expert assistance, I thank the reference staffs of both the Boston Public Library and of the Boston Athenaeum. For their generosity, I am particularly grateful to Howard and Betty Whiteside.

For their help in providing illustrations from the *Hsü ch'a ching*, I thank Dr. Warren Tsuneishi, chief of the Division of Orientalia at the Library of Congress, and Dr. K. T. Wu, head of the Chinese and Korean Section.

I acknowledge also with special thanks the work of Mr. George M. Cushing, photographer, and want to express my gratitude to both him and his assistant, Mr. John J. Simmons, for their concerned professionalism.

Finally, I thank Mr. Van Jay Symons for his interest and bibliographic questings in my behalf; Mr. Shih-ying Woo for his special contribution on the pronunciation of tea and Mr. Robert Gardella for his bibliographic advice. I should also like to thank a friend, who wishes to remain anonymous, for her help with the Latin translations.

I have done my best to provide a smooth translation and to adhere closely to the language of the original. There were many times when those two ends seemed to be contradictory. When such was the case, I have opted for as smooth a translation as possible consonant with the *intent* of the original.

The system of Romanization used is the Wade-Giles

system. The decision to use that system was a function of its still widespread use despite the appearance of better and easier schemes. Place names have also been rendered in the Wade-Giles Romanization. Exceptions to that rule are those places well known in the West under different names, e.g., Canton (Kuang Chou). In such cases, I have used the traditional western renderings. I have attempted to locate places down to the prefectural level. Exceptions are those places so well known in the West that it seemed gratuitous to offer further identification.

Some of the illustrations (the utensils) are inspired by the illustrations in the *Hsü ch'a ching (Supplement to the Classic of Tea)*. They are, however, in every case a product of Miss Hitz's own vision and are quite distinctively her own creation.